Hannah Keeley's

TOTAL MOM MAKEOVER

Also by **Hannah Keeley**

Hannah's Art of Home

Hannah Keeley's

TOTAL MOM MAKEVER

The Six-Week Plan
to Completely Transform
Your Home, Health, Family, and Life

LITTLE, BROWN AND COMPANY

NEW YORK • BOSTON • LONDON

Little, Brown and Company
Hachette Book Group USA
237 Park Avenue, New York, NY 10169
Visit our Web site at www.HachetteBookGroupUSA.com

First Edition: April 2007

The information herein is not intended to replace the services of trained healthcare professionals or be a substitute for medical advice. You are advised to consult with your healthcare professional with regard to matters relating to your health, and in particular regarding matters that may require diagnosis or medical attention.

Library of Congress Cataloging-in-Publication Data
Keeley, Hannah.
    Hannah Keeley's total mom makeover : the six-week plan to completely transform your home, health, family, and life / Hannah Keeley.
        p. cm.
    Includes index.
    ISBN 978-0-316-01719-0
1. Mothers — Psychology.   2. Mothers — Attitudes.
3. Self-esteem in women.   4. Parenting.   5. Home economics.
6. Infants — Care — Handbooks, manuals, etc.   I.   Title.
II.   Title: Total mom makeover.
    HQ759.K42 2007
    646.70085'2 — dc22   2006031131

10 9 8 7 6 5 4 3 2 1

Q-MART
Book design by Fearn Cutler de Vicq
Printed in the United States of America

This book is dedicated to Him,

To him,

To my seven dwarves,

And to all of those beautiful mommies who make this world a better place for the people they love and enable the people they love to better this world.

Contents

Hannah Keeley's

TOTAL MOM MAKEOVER

One Mom's Makeover

I caught a glimpse of myself in the mirror as I walked by with a basket full of laundry fresh out of the dryer. My hair was pulled back in the same scrunchie that I had worn to bed. My face, pale and washed out, had not seen a dab of makeup since last Sunday, and the drab gray sweatshirt that I wore only accentuated the fact that I still had twenty-five pounds to lose. But who has time to shower and dress when you have a house to clean and three kids to look after? And even if I did have time, what was the point?

That's what I told myself.

I walked into my bedroom to dump the laundry on top of the mountain of clean clothes that needed to be folded and put away, and saw clutter all over the floor, cups stacked on the furniture, and tissues wadded up and thrown beside the bed. That's when it hit me. This was not the life I had anticipated.

I was overweight and out of shape. I puffed away on my asthma inhaler day and night and barely managed to keep up with my kids. My complexion was dull, my hair was neglected, and I had abandoned my fashion sense after that first pregnancy test turned out positive. I rationalized that the demands of my home and kids were so consuming that I had no time for myself. But the truth was that every aspect of my life, including my homemaking and mothering, was scattered and disorganized.

The finances were a mess. Bills were stacked up, and a mountain of credit card debt was growing. My home was cluttered. My health was compromised. My days were boring and routine. I had no money, no excitement, no energy, and, worst of all, no motivation. I had totally and completely let myself go — and had taken my home and family with me in the process.

I threw myself down on the floor and cried, and continued sobbing for about five minutes, until I came to a stark realization: No one was coming to rescue me. I was alone with the life that I had created. I loved my babies; there was no question there. But they deserved more. I loved my husband and knew that he deserved more as well. I had resigned myself to a life that I had never imagined, a life that left me with knots in my stomach and a deep longing in my heart.

A false reality had imprisoned me. I believed that the people who looked good, felt good, lived in big houses, made lots of money, and seemed to have their lives together were somehow set apart. They were born into it, the lucky ones. Of course, there were the select few who had made it to the top scratching and clawing, but I comforted myself with the thought that they couldn't be truly happy. Their priorities were definitely out of whack. I could take one look in the mirror and see that my priorities were in place. It was evident in my appearance, my attitude, and even my posture that I put myself dead last. After all, isn't that what a good mother is supposed to do?

But this philosophy just wasn't holding water. If my priorities were in place, then why was my life such a wreck? Why was I so miserable? Why did I wake up feeling tired and go to bed feeling frustrated? Why did I feel this desperate ache for something more? It wasn't just my children and my husband who deserved more. I deserved more! I deserved to feel good, look good, and live up to my full potential.

And that is just what I began to do.

I wiped off my face with a hand towel from the basket of laundry, stood up, and started making improvements in my life. I began meeting my basic needs so that I could think beyond the urgency of the moment. I began to get my life, home, and finances straight so that I could free myself from chaos and frustration. I started focusing on nurturing myself as well as nurturing others, reaching in while also reaching out. Slowly but surely, I began to feel that surge of excitement that comes with competence. I started to trust in myself, and my confidence soared. Eventually I began living up to my true destiny. That amazing woman hidden deep within my own insecurities was now running the show.

But it didn't happen in an instant. It happened with little steps, daily efforts, and moment-by-moment decisions. The efforts multiplied, my strength and self-esteem grew, and the life that was once boring and unsatisfying was now fulfilling and exciting on all levels.

Today, I am glowing. I walk with powerful steps because my life now has direction. My children are whole and happy, my husband admires and respects me, and I am living my dreams. I wake up excited and go to bed feeling content. I am living the life that was intended for me. And it didn't take magic, just a makeover that works!

Where Are You?

Are you ready for something more? Whether you are feeling a bit frustrated or completely overwhelmed by your life right now, I understand. It's time to make some changes. And these changes can begin today. Are you ready to look your best and feel full of energy? Is it time to create a home that is nurturing and fulfilling? Do you want a family life that is fun and supportive? Are you ready to achieve success in every area of your life? If so, then this is the moment to make a conscious decision to go after your goals and follow your dreams. Achieving success as a Total Mom has but one requirement: You've got to want it! If you have the desire, then the life you want to live is already within reach.

What's a Total Mom?

A Total Mom is a woman who is changing the face of homemaking and motherhood. Caring for her home and family is not something she does on the side. It is a priority for her, and she loves what she does. She is smart, energetic, powerful, confident, balanced, and sexy. She doesn't sit around and wait for things to happen. She *makes* things happen!

Although this program focuses on full-time home managers, it is certainly not restricted to them. We live in a time when we can balance a career and a family. I consider myself a full-time home manager even though I also run my own business. It is about the focus, not the title. So whether managing a home and a family is your only career or your most important career, you will definitely benefit from the Total Mom Makeover.

How Does It Work?

The Total Mom Makeover is based on understanding and meeting a mom's needs, from the most basic needs, such as food, shelter, and sex, on up to the higher needs, such as fulfilling your destiny and living up to your potential. You don't just *deserve* a wonderful life, you *need* it. You have only one shot at living the life of your dreams, so make it count.

Back in 1943, a psychologist named Abraham Maslow presented his famous hierarchy of needs. This framework showed different levels of needs, beginning with the most basic, physical needs and moving to higher, more developed needs. His theory contends that as average individuals meet basic needs, such as food and shelter, they seek to satisfy successively higher needs, such as love, trust, and personal growth.

But a mom is not your average individual. She would pull every tooth out of her head if it meant her child would never have a cavity and would gladly sleep in a tent in the Mojave as long as her child was tucked away safe and warm in a Queen Anne bed. She is often so focused on the needs of others that she neglects her own or meets them in unhealthy and unfulfilling ways. This sets her up for failure and dissatisfaction down the road. And it's not just the mom who suffers. If she is running on empty, then she has nothing to give. Every person who depends on her and every obligation that she carries will suffer as well.

A mom's needs must be met in a way that takes into account all of her other responsibilities. She is not isolated in her mental, physical, and emotional development, for it directly affects every plate that she

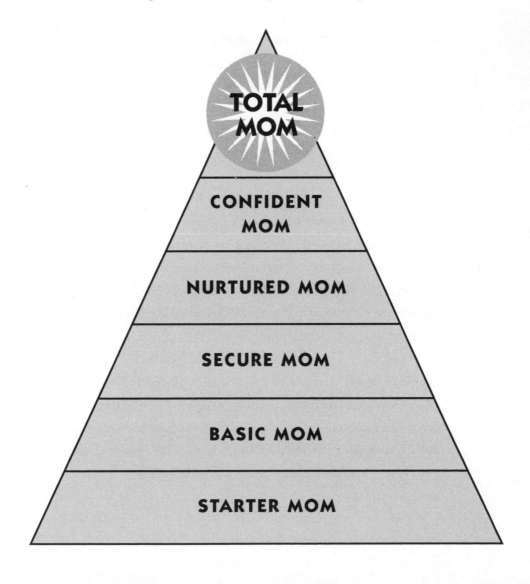

spins and every life that she touches. If she is healthy, then her home and family reflect that. If she is unhealthy, then her home and family reflect that, too. Therefore, the Total Mom Makeover is not just for mom but for every person and every thing she cares about.

The Total Mom Needs Pyramid shown on the previous page is a perfect illustration of how a mom develops in a healthy, whole manner by first meeting her basic needs and then progressing in her personal development. Building a healthy foundation will launch her toward living a more productive and fulfilling life on all levels.

The Total Mom Makeover takes six weeks, five days a week, for a total of thirty days. Each week is dedicated to one level on the Total Mom Needs Pyramid. Each day, you will read out of this book, do some exercises in a journal, and put what you have learned into practice. On the weekends you will continue to grow through the Weekend Workouts. Here is a breakdown of what you can expect to accomplish each week.

Week One: Starter Mom

You will tear down that faulty pyramid that you may be working with in order to build a stronger, more successful one. You will also acquire the tools you need to construct a better life. You will learn how to develop a vision, how to make every motion and moment count, how to speak your way to success, and how to develop a winning attitude.

Week Two: Basic Mom

With the right tools in place, you will begin meeting your basic needs in the healthiest and most enriching ways possible, building a foundation for growth. You will learn how to eliminate toxins from your diet, clutter from your home, and boredom from your sex life. You will also develop your own inner fashionista and learn key strategies to increase your energy level.

Week Three: Secure Mom

With your basic needs met, you will move on to free yourself from the fear and uncertainty that tomorrow often holds and to establish a sense of security in your life. You will learn how to plug up those leaks in your wallet and to work exercise into your daily routine. You will also develop methods to manage your temper as well as your housekeeping responsibilities.

Week Four: Nurtured Mom

With your security intact, you will work on your love and relationship needs. You will be nurtured not only through your relationships with friends and family but also through your relationship with yourself. You will learn how to make mealtime special and how to create a nurturing home. You will also develop key strategies to make your marriage work.

Week Five: Confident Mom

Being fully nurtured, you will focus on meeting your needs for personal esteem and competence in all areas of your life. You will learn to trust your inner voice and pursue your destiny. You will develop muscles in your body and organization throughout your home. You will also learn some beauty secrets that will boost your confidence as well as your appearance.

Week Six: Total Mom

With confidence in your spirit, you can move on to living the Total Mom life. You will fine-tune those attitude skills and experience life to the fullest. You will learn how to meet your children's basic needs as well as your own personal need for solitude. You will also develop techniques to help you keep up the life that you have created.

How to Use This Book

The Total Mom Makeover will radically improve your life, but only if you put in the maximum effort. In other words, you get out of it what you put into it. Here's how to get the most bang for your buck:

Step One: Get a journal. This can be a nice hardcover book full of blank paper or even just a spare notebook you have lying around. You will use this every day for the next six weeks, and it will be invaluable. At the end of each day, you will complete a few exercises in your journal. Doing this will help you make incredible progress, and you'll be able to look back on it later to see how far you have come.

Step Two: Set aside a specific time each morning to read through that day's section in this book. If you wake up early enough to give yourself about thirty minutes of uninterrupted time in the morning, it may very well turn into your favorite time of day. Early morning is a perfect time to focus on growth and change.

Step Three: Get excited about what you are doing and how far you are going to go. And be patient with yourself. Some days will be great, but there will be others when you feel as if you are swimming upstream. But you *can* do this, and you *will* make progress every day.

Can You Handle the Truth?

The truth is that you may very well be living a life that is far below your potential. Many people get to the end of their life and realize they have only lived a tenth of it. I don't want this for you, and I know, by the sheer fact that you are reading this book, that you don't want this for yourself. You want to live a full life, an abundant life. You want to get to the end of your day and know that you squeezed as much juice out of it as possible. And once you start tapping into the passion and power that lies within, you will be amazed at what you can accomplish.

Let me go ahead and tell you this: Just by having the desire to get more out of life and wanting to manage your home and family more effectively, you are already miles ahead of the pack. Most people are more than content to float through life, going wherever the current carries them. You are ready to take control and start designing the life you have always wanted. But enough talk already. Let's get started on this makeover!

STARTER MOM

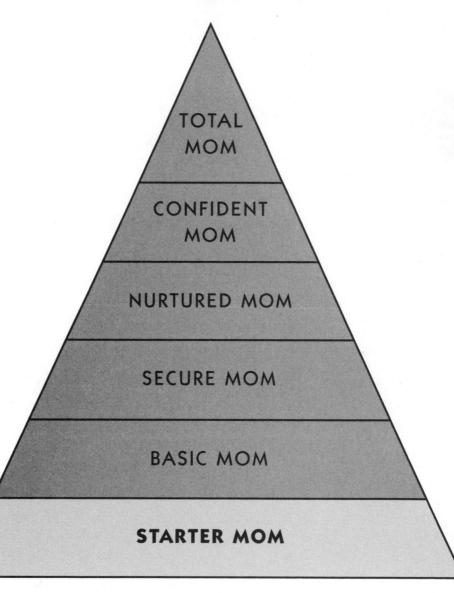

TOTAL
MOM

CONFIDENT
MOM

NURTURED MOM

SECURE MOM

BASIC MOM

STARTER MOM

Get Ready, Get Set

Motherhood has a way of sneaking up on you. One day, you are rubbing cocoa butter on your expanding belly and trying to decide on colors for the curtains in the nursery. The next day, you are wearing sweatpants because you can't button your jeans, dishes are spilling out of the kitchen sink, and the kids have colored all over the walls with permanent markers. Because of the ever-growing list of responsibilities, you begin pushing your own needs further and further down on the list. Eventually, you are just trying to make it through another day without losing your car keys, your temper, or your mind.

That's no way to live. And deep inside, you know that. But you can't stop long enough to catch your breath. And even when you do have a moment, you have no idea how to begin to make it better. Well, the time is now, the place is here, and you're going to start by forgetting everything you know about motherhood.

Old School

Our grandmothers knew how to do motherhood, but that's because they didn't have as many options as we do now. They were raised to know how to cook and clean, how to care for babies, and how to send their husbands off to work with a wink and a smile. They were smart women who applied themselves to their homes and families. They also knew that they were only as strong as their support network, so they reached out and maintained a sense of community with other moms.

Our mothers had more options but an entirely new set of challenges. They were brave women treading new territory in their careers and personal accomplishments. But they still had homes and families to care for, so their lives became a struggle as they learned to balance their responsibilities. With the advantages came the disadvantages. Even the mothers who chose to make family their primary career felt left behind as their support network donned business suits and left for work.

That was then. This is now.

Moms today have options that our grandmothers could never have imagined. We can choose to stay at home, go to work, or even work from home so that we can build a career as well as a family. We can raise our kids and even educate our kids, build a career or pursue a hobby, invest in our marriages while investing in ourselves. It is truly a great time to be a mom, a time full of possibilities and opportunities. As a matter of fact, there are so many options today that it is often difficult to make a choice.

Therein lies the problem: How do we choose? We have a family to care for and a home to manage, but there are endless other choices to be made. We have instant access to entertainment and community through computers, televisions, and telephones. We can shop from our homes or our closest mall. We can take our kids to gym class, the park, the living room, or even to work with us. It's no longer a question of what we have to choose from, but how we make our choices. This determines whether we sink or swim.

New World, New Strategy

The old strategies won't cut it in the world of mommyhood any longer. It's not how quickly we can wash the dishes or how balanced we can make our family meals that matters so much today. What matters is how we choose to invest our time, money, and energy in order to build a successful and healthy home, family, and life. So forget what you know about motherhood. If it's not working, throw it out.

The first step to becoming a Total Mom is to forget about what you *should* be doing. The *should*s keep you running around like crazy, fueling everyone and everything while you dwindle down to nothing. So quit beating yourself up. There is no room in the Total Mom life for negativity and self-sabotage. Just take it one step at a time. It's not about what you *should* be doing. It's about what you *could* be doing. This could be the time of your life to really shine and discover all of the enormous potential that is buried within you. Quit feeling guilty. Quit feeling powerless. Quit feeling hopeless. You don't have time for that anymore. Throw out the old and usher in the new.

TOTAL MOM TIP
"Shoulds, Coulds, and Woulds, Oh My!"

Okay, maybe you *should* be spending less money, getting in shape, raising your children better. You *could* be doing that. Or you *would* be doing that *if only*. The truth of the *should*s, *could*s, and *would*s is that they do nothing productive for you. Instead they torment you mentally and rob you of valuable time and energy. *Should*s, *could*s, and *would*s dwell in some far-off world out in the middle of nowhere. *Can* and *will* exist right here, right now. If you find yourself wasting time by dwelling in the *should*s of life, then leave those words behind you. Repeat to yourself, *"I can"* or *"I will"* and move forward to take some productive action. Staring at your thighs in the mirror and regretting those Double Stuf Oreos will do nothing for you. Instead, say, *"I will* work on these thighs," and go do twenty reps of leg lifts. No more guilt. It's time to take action.

Have You Reached a Decision?

Don't waste your time any longer by wishing, hoping, or heaping on the guilt. If you are ever going to achieve any level of success, it must start with a conscious decision. I'm not talking about a fly-by-night whim. I'm talking about a true-blue decision, one of those moments when you close all other doors except the one you are walking through. When I was sobbing on the floor of my bedroom, physically, financially, and emotionally impoverished, I made a conscious decision to improve my life. There were no other options.

Moods will come and go, but a true decision sticks with you no matter what. It's a "for better" or "for worse" commitment. It's easy to make a decision to lose fifteen pounds when you just finished off a bowl of ice cream dripping in hot fudge. But when everyone around you is munching on nachos and you haven't eaten anything except some rice cakes and a bowl of minestrone soup, it gets pretty difficult to stick to your guns. A real decision has the power to stick with you — even through the nachos.

TOTAL MOM TIP
**Share
the News!**

Commit yourself to this makeover by telling someone about it, such as a close friend or relative. Make sure she is tough enough to hold you responsible for your commitment and motivate you along the way. By sharing your decision, you have taken an action to fulfill it, and this is a huge step.

Sometimes a decision is easy to make because you see no other alternative. Or perhaps you do see that alternative and it scares your pants off. I saw what I was becoming, that day on the floor, and the decision to improve was an easy one. Take a look at the path ahead of you. Does it lead to success or cycle back through dissatisfaction and personal failure? If you are headed for success, then I hope this program is just more steam in your engine. If you are not headed in that direction, then you are standing at a crossroads. You need to be the one to make the decision that you deserve more. Today can be the day to take a different path.

Go For It!

True decisions have power behind them. They are not idle wishes or weak hopes. They are commitments that are set in stone. Forget about saying "I *wish* I had a nicer home" or "I would *like* to be healthier." These are little wisps of yearnings that evaporate into thin air. A true decision comes with a launchpad underneath. "I *will create* a nicer home." "I *will take steps* to become healthier." These use action verbs—*massive* action verbs! A true decision leads you down a determined path, with no option of turning back. It pushes you beyond your current point into an entirely new reality.

Life truly can change in an instant. Today you can make a decision that will affect your entire outcome. You can begin right now to create your new reality. Envision the life that you want to live, leave everything behind, and go after it. If you know deep inside that there has got to be more to life, then you are right on track. Use your dissatisfaction to propel you to new levels of achievement. This makeover will give you the strategies you need to live the life you deserve, so make that decision—*now!*

Week One, Day One: Daily Exercises

1. Leave the past where it belongs. This is a new day, with a fresh start. In your Total Mom Makeover journal, date the first page and write "Week One, Day One." You will label each day of this makeover in the same way, with the appropriate week and day. Now think about all of those *should*s that you have been carrying around with you—everything that bugs you about your home, health, family, and life—and write them down. These can be anything from "I should spend more time playing with the kids" to "I should keep a cleaner house." Whatever it is that's bugging you, this is the time to get it out of your head and onto paper. Take as long as you like and empty out all of the burdens you have been carrying around. Don't worry about doing anything about them now. That will come later.

2. Are you ready to embark on this six-week journey? Make a firm decision that you want more out of life, that you want to be the best mother, wife, homemaker, and woman that you could ever be. Now set this decision in stone by writing it down in your journal. Begin with "I have decided . . . " and finish the sentence according to what you desire for your home, your health, your family, and your life. It can be just a few sentences, or it can take up an entire page. After you finish, you may want to log on to TotalMom.com and join the Total Mom Makeover Club. You'll be glad you did.

Check Your Vision

The more I strive for success in my personal and professional life, the more I realize that the world will get out of the way for a person with unshakable vision. By *vision,* I don't mean an idealistic view of what you would like to see happen someday. I mean the kind of vision that wakes you up in the morning and starts your engine, the kind of vision that is so real you can almost taste it. That's the kind of vision you need to have as a mother. You need to see the mom that you want to become with such acute clarity that you will adopt that character as your own.

Greased Lightning

You've probably seen the movie *Grease.* In one part, The T-Birds are faced with the challenge of turning a broken-down hunk of junk into a streamlined, powered-up race car. Most of the boys are laughing about the horrible condition of the car and mocking the task, but Danny Zuko, played by John Travolta, decides to open their eyes to the possibilities. He begins by saying, "This car could be automatic, systematic, hydromatic. Why, it could be Greased Lightning!" Suddenly, they all break out into a song-and-dance number while they create a fantastic, shining, glimmering car, complete with silver lightning bolts painted along the body and a pair of fluffy dice hanging from the rearview mirror. The dance number ends with everyone gathered around the car and Zuko on top of the glistening creation. Then the car turns back into the junk heap that they had before, with everyone in the same position around it. Zuko looks around, shouts, "Let's get to work!" and jumps down. Nothing happened with the car. But a remarkable thing happened with the T-Birds. They now had a vision; and the vision was strong enough to put them to work.

What Is a Vision?

I have found that most people have a very distorted idea of what a vision really is. They see it as a daydream or fantasy. They would rather tune in to the Fine Living or Entertainment channel to see how the rich and famous live than pour energy into their own lives. For many, a vision is an escape from reality. However, the truth is that a real vision is a powerful tool that can help you create the reality you desire. If you can truly envision it, then you can realize it.

I opened up a fortune cookie once, and the words on that little slip of paper have always stayed with me: "One person dreamed of becoming somebody. Another remained awake and became." I don't remember what I ate, and I don't even recall the restaurant, but I will always remember that fortune. Visions can build us up or tear us down. If your vision is just a form of escape, then all it will do is lead you down a white rabbit's hole. Daydreaming is never a waste of time as long as it is being used as a tool, not an escape route. Our daydreams help us to create visions of the family life we want to live, the body we want to have, the house we want to own. These daydreams are healthy as long as they continue to move us forward. If your daydreams pull you away from reality, they eat up time and energy that you could put toward realizing your dreams.

However, let me give you a word of warning. When you begin making progress, the world will fight you tooth and nail. Fighting the inertia in order to pursue your vision will probably be the most challenging task when it comes to achieving your goals. As soon as you decide that you want to be a kinder, more compassionate mother, your child will publicly embarrass you and make you boiling mad. When you make a resolution to catch up on your laundry, the washing machine will break and flood half of the house. On the day you decide to get in shape, your neighbor will appear at your door with a platter of fudge. It's inevitable. But it's not impossible. The way I see it, the more obstacles I overcome, the more skills I develop. A true vision is not a guarantee against pitfalls. Instead, it is a reason to find a way to scrape, scratch, and claw your way out of them.

The Mom You Want to Be

What is your vision? Today is the day when you bring that into focus. If you want to change your life, it all begins with a clear vision of the direction in which you're headed. It works like this: Visualize the future and then begin making adjustments in your life to fit that vision. You won't be able to get fit until you can visualize yourself with more muscle tone and less fat, looking hot in all of your clothes. You won't get your home organized until you can imagine it in operation with all of its systems in place. Today you need to get a clear picture of the Total Mom that you want to become.

We are all in a process of becoming, and as soon as you feel as if you have "arrived," a new challenge usually pops up. Life is a learning experience, but you have to be the one to initiate growth and change in response to that learning. You can easily fall into a cycle of existence where your days meld together and you feel as if you are treading water. But if you have a clear vision of your goals and your future, then transformation is always taking place. Every day, every moment, can be a move forward and upward if you have a clear vision in place.

"Your vision will become clear only when you look into your heart. Who looks outside, dreams. Who looks inside, awakens."
—CARL JUNG

Make It Tangible

The clearer you can make your vision, the easier it will be for you to make it a reality. For example, if you want to look and feel healthier, then visualize that woman with all of your senses. Hear how she breathes while she exercises, see the muscular definition in her arms and thighs, taste the healthy whole foods that she chooses to eat, feel how the clothes fit her body. See it and feel it with such clarity and conviction that you make it your new reality.

Your mind truly cannot tell the difference between what you clearly imagine and what you actually do. You activate the exact same neural process when you see yourself shooting a basketball through a hoop in your imagination and when you actually do it with your body. The mind is remarkable. What we imagine, we become.

Every day, take a moment and focus on the clear and tangible vision of the woman you are becoming. Take a moment and focus on becoming her. Walk like her, talk like her, speak to the children like her, love your husband like her. She is the new you.

Don't Accept Less than the Best

You deserve the very best in life: the best home, the best family, the best husband. You deserve to look good and feel good. You deserve to be positive, inspired, energetic, and excited every day. You deserve to cram fifty lifetimes' worth of living into your one life. This is, or will be, your reality. And everything that does not fit into this reality is considered subpar and unacceptable. Our lives are completely determined by what we will and will not accept.

So what are you accepting right now? What are you begrudgingly living with day after day? If you feel that aspects of your life are subpar, are you content to let them remain that way? Have you reached the point where you refuse to accept anything less than what is best for you? You were meant for great and mighty things, but they will only happen in your life when you are ready to accept them as your reality.

What you believe about yourself is a self-fulfilling prophecy. If you tell yourself that a prosperous future is just not in the cards for you, then you have made that reality inevitable. You are the only one holding the cards. No power on earth—money, looks, luck, talent, opportunity, nothing—can stand up against the power of your beliefs and your determination to act in accordance with those beliefs.

Week One, Day Two: Daily Exercises

1. Look at the list of *should*s that you made yesterday. You will probably find that most of the things you listed are areas where you feel the greatest amount of dissatisfaction. Use this list as a springboard to identify what you want out of life. Take those frustrations and channel them to create a clear vision of the woman that you want to become. Label and date the next page in your journal and write "My Vision" across the top. Now describe this new woman. Own this vision by writing it in the first person and get as illustrative as possible with your description. How do you act? Dress? Speak? For example, "I have boundless energy. I eat healthy food that nourishes my body. I look sexy in my stylish clothes. I smile at my children and flirt with my husband." This is the new you! Make your description as clear as possible so that you can carry this vision around with you at all times.

2. Women are often very visually perceptive. Use this attribute to your advantage. Look through your favorite magazines and books to find pictures and quotes that capture the vision that you have for your home, health, family, and life. Glue these pictures on the next clean two-page spread in your journal so that the illustrations cover both pages. Leave some blank spots to fill in as the vision evolves.

WEEK ONE, DAY THREE

Words That Work

Words carry with them a mighty force. Believe it or not, all of us possess magical powers, and we can choose to use these powers for evil or for good. We perform magical incantations every day, using words to hurt and to heal, to push forward and to pull back. If you can harness this power, there is no limit to the magic you can perform, both in your life and in the lives of others.

Casting Spells

My two oldest children are die-hard *Harry Potter* fans. When they were younger, they would pretend that they were students at Hogwarts. They fashioned wands out of sticks and learned all of the magic spells. I would often hear them casting spells on each other. "Petrificus Totalus!"—and all of a sudden the opponent would be frozen solid. "Tarantallegra!"—and the other person's legs would begin dancing uncontrollably. They were pretending, of course, but the magic of words is just that tangible. Words can immobilize us, and words can make our lives a beautiful dance. They have unbelievable power.

When you voice something, you give it a life and the permission to exist. Our words often dictate our behaviors and the behaviors of others. For example, in the learning room of my house I have a list of rules on

26

the wall. One of the rules is pretty obvious—it's the word *can't* with a big slash mark through it. None of the children are allowed to say *can't* when referring to their abilities. By saying you can't do something, you have already defeated yourself. A math problem or a vocabulary word doesn't have the power to defeat you; only you have the power to defeat you. And when you use limiting words, you are limiting yourself.

Black Magic, White Magic

It's not just what we say but also what we hear that affects our lives in powerful ways. Positive comments can propel us to new levels of greatness; negative comments have the potential to scar us for life. I don't know if you have any toxic spells infecting your life, but many of us walk around with verbal curses shadowing our pathways. Perhaps someone close to you has told you, "You're not smart enough," "You don't have what it takes," or "Don't get your hopes up." Little curses can work black magic over our lives, just as real as if a sorcerer waved his wand and cast a spell. These toxic words infect your entire existence. They put up parameters where there should be unlimited potential, and they need to be wiped away. You have the power to perform your own white magic.

When you feel those past comments striking you down, be armed with your own quiver of white magic arrows to shoot each one—a blessing for each curse. For example, if you have been told you are not smart and those words continue to haunt you, then give yourself a positive message: "I am a smart woman. I am intelligent and creative." Positive messages drain these curses of the spell that they have cast over you. Curses and blessings have no power other than the power that you ascribe to them. How much do you believe in the negative messages that have been given to you? Maybe it's time to develop a new reality—a belief in the potential that lies within you. When you give yourself positive messages, believe them. Make them real, say them out loud, support them with your actions. If you believe you are smart, intelligent, and creative, then

"Words—so innocent and powerless as they are, as standing in a dictionary, how potent for good and evil they become in the hands of one who knows how to combine them."
—NATHANIEL HAWTHORNE

you will act accordingly. You will read quality literature. You will act on your creative ideas. You will engage in stimulating conversation. Words are powerful, but it is your belief in those words that will determine your response.

Power Up Your Vocabulary

You can transform your world when you transform your vocabulary. Whether we realize it or not, the words we say carry a lot of weight. Begin to consider your words carefully before you utter them. Start minimizing your negative comments and maximizing your positive ones. Once, I felt very ill. Evidently I was battling some kind of bug that was going around. But I would never say that I was sick. To me, *sick* carried too many negative connotations. When my husband, Blair, would ask how I felt, I would reply with something like, "I'm feeling a bit challenged," or maybe, "I'm just a tad uncomfortable." Finally, he said, "Would you just admit that you're sick?"

Detox Your Mommy Vocabulary

TOXIC PHRASES	PHRASES WITH POTENTIAL
"sick and tired"	"reached a decision"
"completely overwhelmed"	"somewhat challenged"
"I'm disappointed in you."	"I'm surprised at your behavior."
"getting on my nerves"	"helping me stretch"
"I can't take it anymore."	"I'm growing."
"You know better!"	"Let me teach you."
"I'm so depressed."	"I need some motivation."
"I have failed."	"I have learned."

It may seem ludicrous to some, but I really do believe that there is power in the words you use to describe your situation. You can feel angry, or you can feel a bit put off. You can feel happy, or you can feel overjoyed. The use of powerful words can actually put you into a more powerful state. Try it today and see for yourself. Be selective about the words that you choose. Make sure that the toxic words are leaving your vocabulary and that you are replacing them with words that are strong and instrumental in helping you get what you want out of life. Toxic words imply that there is no change possible, but words that carry potential suggest that there is room for improvement. I hear a lot of "mommy talk" in my circles, and unfortunately a large amount of it is toxic. Begin taking measures today to replace those phrases with something less negative. You will find that it really does make a difference.

The Language of Love

I have found that when it comes to our homes, we loosen our belts a bit and let our hair down. What we would never say in public comes spilling out of our lips when we are safe at home. I have heard moms chastise their children terribly in public, and I can't help thinking, *If she is saying that here in public, then I'm scared to think of how she speaks to her children at home.* Of all places to foster enriching speech, the home should be at the top of the list.

Our children are absorbing everything we do and say. Don't just think about what you are feeding their bodies; consider what you are feeding their minds. Let the words that you direct toward them, as well as toward your husband, be words that lift up instead of tear down. They need healthy food to build strong bodies, and they need healthy words to build strong spirits. There will be enough in the world to challenge their confidence. It is your job to create unshakable character through the words that you choose. Eliminate the toxic phrases but also look for opportunities to feed them with words and phrases that enrich and empower. "You did it!" "You are so smart!" "You amaze me!" "I am astounded at how incredible you are!" These words act like building blocks, creating strength and competence. And the opportunities to build them up are always there.

I remember once, two of my boys were having a difficult time getting along. They would either bicker over toys or ignore each other. I finally decided to conduct my own experiment in shaping reality. I began talking to them about how great they played together, about how happy it made me to see how much they loved each other. I even made a point of talking to other people about them when I knew the boys were close by so they could hear me gushing over how wonderfully they got along. (Hint: Kids always listen more carefully when they overhear something.) In other words, I began speaking the reality that I wanted instead of the one that I was currently faced with. Remember, in order to shape your beliefs, you create a reality and then step into it as if it already exists. I created the reality that I wanted (my two boys getting along) and then started behaving as if it were already in effect. And the results were amazing. Within days, they began playing together and enjoying each other. After about a week, I overheard my older son talking in the other room, and when I peeked in, I saw him reading a book to his little

TOTAL MOM TIP
Speak to
Their Spirits

I learned a little trick from my oldest sister, Regina, that I would love to pass along. When you are taking your children to the bathroom in the middle of the night, when you are rocking them to sleep, or when you are simply planting a kiss on their sleeping faces, you have a great opportunity to speak to their subconscious. Their minds are processing so many things, and they are actually absorbing the words that they hear even though they can't respond. Speak to them and speak about them in beautiful, positive ways. Tell them how wonderful they are, how they are going to change the world, how much you love and adore them. These words are like sweet nectar to their spirits, building them up from the inside out.

brother. The transformation was incredible, and it testifies to the power of the words we speak. As a mom, you have the power to shape your children's world, so choose your words wisely.

Ask Yourself THE Question

The way you communicate with others is extremely powerful. The way others communicate with you can also be powerful. But by far, the most powerful communication occurs within. Master the art of self-communication and you can master your life. You can train yourself to make decisions that will strengthen you and help you reach that vision you have for yourself.

We all have a tendency to do things that keep us from reaching our goals. You stuff your face when you want to lose weight. You sleep in when you want to get a head start on your day. You yell at your kids when you want to be compassionate. This happens when you lose focus of your vision. If your vision could stay clear, then your actions would be in line with your ultimate desires. By harnessing the power of self-communication, you can maintain your focus and make the decisions necessary to reach your goal. So forget all of the negative stuff you have heard about talking to yourself. Start communicating today by asking yourself this question —

"What do I *really* want?"

This question will help you gain your focus even when the fog is closing in. We stuff our faces because we listen to our stomachs and not our heads. We sleep in because we let our eyes close instead of putting our feet on the floor. We yell at our kids because our tempers rise and our patience wears thin. But in all of these situations, if you could step back for just a moment and ask yourself, "What do I *really* want?" you would be able to gain focus and act in accordance with your goals. You would realize that you *really* want to feel thin instead of stuffed. You *really* want to get ahead instead of behind. You *really* want to love your children instead of frustrate them. This question will help you put things into perspective when you need it the most.

Practice asking yourself this question, especially when that sneaky voice within tempts you to settle for less and give in to complacency instead of putting forth that extra effort that could make all the difference. Ask yourself out loud, "What do I *really* want?" After you ask it, visualize it. See what you really want for your life. If you are tempted to leave that clutter all over the floor, visualize what the room looks like when it is clean and neat. Focus on the goal that you want to achieve and see yourself acting in accordance with that goal. Hear it. See it. Act on it.

We live in surroundings that tempt us. We long for something better, but our bodies and minds continually desire instant gratification. Remember that the instant road never leads to ultimate fulfillment. True satisfaction lies in living in accordance with your ultimate desires—a fulfilling home, a happy family, a healthy body and mind, and a joyful existence. The skill of communication can help you reach that true satisfaction. It can help you keep your focus. Yes, words can work magic. In every word you speak, and in every word that you choose to listen to, you are either building up or tearing down. Speak with love and power, hear words that support and encourage, talk to yourself constantly, and start getting what you really, *really* want out of life.

Week One, Day Three: Daily Exercises

1. Write down the four categories in your journal—Home, Health, Family, and Life. Under each one, give yourself a positive and empowering message that encompasses the vision that you have developed. Write these messages down and speak them out loud throughout the day. For example, simply saying, "I love my home," can completely transform your attitude and your family's attitude

about the house that you live in. Take each message and post it where you will see it every day. Reading the words "I am a beautiful woman who is creating a life that I love" when you look in the bathroom mirror is a fantastic way to begin each day!

2. Think about some of the negative phrases or words that you may be using around your kids. Hopefully, you are not using any profanity, but if so, then by all means include that as well. Write these down, and next to each one, write down a new word or phrase that carries potential with it. Practice using these replacements so that you can eliminate poisonous words from your vocabulary.

Take Action

Every mom has twenty-four hours in a day, so why is it that some can accomplish ten or twenty times what others can? Why is it that one woman can take care of a family of nine while another can barely survive with only two? Or one mom can hold a part-time job and keep a clean home while another can't even find time to make her bed? Some people have learned the skill of getting more accomplished in less time, and it all boils down to taking action. Our life takes shape when we get going and begin shaping it. Today you will learn to apply skills to reach your goals.

Action Skill #1: Piggyback Your Tasks

Task management for moms is vastly different from task management for other professionals. We have to develop our minds to see little pockets of opportunity and take full advantage of them. When we take a minute to use the bathroom, we can wipe off the counter after we wash our hands. When we walk through the living room, we can pick up four toys on our way. When we clean off the dining room table, we can bag up the trash as well. We can take multitasking to an entirely new level, making it look more like an art form than a coping mechanism.

You can easily double or triple your accomplishments when you learn how to piggyback your tasks. Make it a game to see how much you can complete in one singular effort by doing two or three tasks on the way to accomplishing another. For example, as you pick up toys in the living room, why not de-clutter a bit by tossing some in a bag to give away to charity? When you fill up the car with gas, why not collect some trash from the car and throw it away while you are at the station?

Everyone has a to-do list somewhere. Start looking over your list and see how many tasks you can piggyback. Can you pick up the weekly groceries on your way to take a child to a music lesson? Can you prepare those cookies for the class party while you are making a casserole for dinner? And since you are already making a casserole, can you go ahead and make two more and freeze them for later? Start looking for opportunities to piggyback and make the best use of those little pockets of time available to you throughout the day.

Action Skill #2: Take Baby Steps

One big fat rule of any improvement program is this: Never ever set yourself up for failure. If you bite off more than you can chew, there is a chance that you will have to spit it out and forget the whole idea. You eat a big salad one little bite at a time. And you reach big goals one small step after another.

A good friend of mine, Kimberly, decided that she wanted to get in shape, so she enlisted the help of another friend who is a competitive runner. They made plans to begin running together the next week. Well, the day arrived, Kimberly put on her new running shoes, and they stretched for a few minutes and hit the pavement. They weren't half a mile down the road when Kimberly exclaimed, "Forget it!" Her body ached, she couldn't breathe, and her stomach was turning flips. She not only gave up on the run, she also gave up on running. The episode was so disappointing that she didn't have the heart to try again. She went for five months without making a single attempt at getting in shape, until one day a glance into a full-length mirror got her motivated once more. The next morning, she decided that she would go on a walk with a bit of running here and there. On her first day out, she walked a mile and ran the distance of, in her words, "a few mailboxes." But this was enough to get her going. She began doing this every morning, walking and running, until she was doing more running than walking. One mile turned into two, which turned into five. Nine months later, Kimberly ran her very first marathon. The tiny efforts really do matter. Like stair steps, they build upon each other and get you where you want to go.

This makeover is composed of baby steps. With every exercise completed, every passage read, and every task accomplished, you are getting closer and closer to that vision that you have for yourself. Some days you will feel like walking; other times you will run full speed ahead. But the most important thing to remember is to keep taking those baby steps, one at a time. Speed is not nearly as important as persistence.

Action Skill #3: Have Fun

When you love what you're doing, chances are you'll keep doing it. When you begin plotting out those baby steps that will help you reach your goals, make sure that you'll enjoy taking them. I know it can be difficult at times. How much fun is scrubbing the toilet or doing thirty sit-ups? But there are ways to make every task more enjoyable. All it takes is a little bit of creativity. Here are some examples to get you started:

- ◉ Don't want to exercise? Put on some favorite tunes that will get you moving and dance around the house with the kids for twenty minutes.
- ◉ Tired of healthy meals? Appeal to the other senses during dinner. Put on entertaining music, light candles, use your finest dishes and stemware.

- Hard time getting out of bed? Buy a special mug that you use for your morning tea or coffee. Spend five minutes stretching and enjoying the solitude.
- Don't feel like cleaning up? Put on some music and make it a game by finishing the task before the end of the song.
- Hate folding clothes? Do all the folding while watching one of your favorite television shows.

Hopefully, these ideas will spur you on to add some fun to the baby steps that you need to take every day. Life is way too short to hate what you do. Love your life! Love what you do! A dose of fun, or as Mary Poppins says, "a spoonful of sugar," will help you enjoy the daily tasks that will lead to your desired goal.

Action Skill #4: Be Selective

One of my best-kept secrets of housekeeping was discovered one day when I had a friend over, and her son, who was playing on the floor with my kids, looked under my sofa and loudly exclaimed, "Mom! Come quick! You'll never believe all of the junk under here!" Yes, it's true. I'm coming clean for the greater cause of helping all moms out there become Total Moms. One clever trick to making people think you do it all is to *not* do it all. Just be selective and do the things that really matter.

But shortcuts are not always easy for perfectionist women (I used to be one—the hangers in my closet were color coded). My advice is to begin working out your slacker muscles with some training exercises. Iron only the parts of a shirt that are going to show, mop only the parts of the floor that are actually dirty, vacuum without moving the furniture, and practice other household tips of the lazy and unmotivated. I know this sounds like odd advice coming from a professional homemaker, but if you can train yourself to do things imperfectly, you will learn to get things done more effectively. If you are only satisfied with perfection,

"I find the great thing in this world is not so much where we stand, as in what direction we are moving: To reach the port of heaven, we must sail sometimes with the wind and sometimes against it, but we must sail, and not drift, nor lie at anchor"
—OLIVER WENDELL HOLMES,
Autocrat of the Breakfast Table

then it is often hard to get motivated enough to complete a task. Don't try to do everything, just the things that really matter. Achieving success in life is as much about prioritizing as it is about getting up the gumption to go after your goals. If you're going to get the important things done, you've got to be able to let lesser things go.

Action Skill #5: Build It in Blocks

This is another one of my tried-and-true tricks. When I know I've got work to do and I have absolutely no motivation, I simply set "blocks" of activity in which to do it. As long as I know that there is some finishing point, it's easy to get the work done. For example, if I need to return e-mails or phone calls, I give myself a time limit, maybe fifteen minutes, to dive into the activity. At the end of that block of time, I can just stop what I'm doing and save the rest for the next day, or if I have enough momentum going, I can just finish the entire list. Getting started is the most difficult part of any task. Get past that, and the rest is a breeze. Blocks help you break down a job into bite-size chunks so you can dig right in. If you have a stack of items to file, then set an activity block for yourself. Perhaps you can file ten items a day. This may seem small, but

BLOCK PARTIES

Cleaning up can be fun and games (all right, maybe just games) when you do it in blocks. Here are some of the Keeley family's most successful block parties:

- Ten-Minute Tidy: Set a timer for ten minutes and have everyone in the family pick up throughout the house until the timer goes off.
- Pick Up by Number: Set a certain number and tell everyone that they need to pick up that many items.
- Cleanup Countdown: Everyone in the family starts with a set number of items, such as five, picks up that many, puts them away, and

you will be shocked at the progress that little "baby blocks" can provide. Moms have a lot to do, but no one ever said we had to do it in one fell swoop.

Action Skill #6: Reward Yourself

There is a reason that a rat makes it through the maze. He knows there is a block of cheese waiting for him at the end. Just like there is a reason I will fold ten loads of laundry in one day: I know there is a luxurious bubble bath waiting for me at the end of it. The Total Mom knows that she's got to be good to herself. Reward your efforts and you'll be more likely to repeat the pattern. We're great with this when it comes to our kids: "You can go outside to play as soon as your room is clean." But in all honesty, we never outgrow this little trick.

Sometimes we just need incentive, so don't be stingy when it comes to doling out the self-rewards. If you cleaned out the linen closet and donated two bags full of sheets and comforters to charity, then reward yourself with a luxurious new sheet set. If you managed to survive as team mom for an entire soccer season, then take an afternoon off and go for a pedicure. Just because you are a mom does not mean that you are

then moves down to four, three, two, and one. This is an evil way to take advantage of less proficient mathematicians, but it works.

- Room Sweep: Give everyone a room or area of the house that they are responsible for (then you know who to blame later).
- Commercial Cleanup: Everyone gets to watch TV, but during commercials they are all required to get up and clean.

Warning: Even though you try to make it as enjoyable as possible, the titles of these games will only serve to nauseate your children later on in life.

serving a prison sentence. Your life is meant to be both productive and enjoyable. So give yourself plenty of treats along the way.

Stock up on some little rewards for yourself and hide them away for days when you feel especially unmotivated. Try to make them as calorie-free as possible, such as a new candle, gourmet tea, a good book, some style mags, or fruit juice Popsicles. One of my friends keeps dark-chocolate-covered espresso beans in her freezer. Each time she finishes a big household task that she especially dreads, she rewards herself with a couple of beans. Hey, whatever works!

TOTAL MOM TIP
Get the Goods!

Action Skill #7: Do It Now

If there is something that needs to be done, then DO IT NOW. Don't waste any more time procrastinating and trying to come up with excuses to dodge the inevitable. If you are going to get your goals accomplished, you need to understand the importance of doing it now. Doing it now means getting maximum results out of every opportunity. If you keep putting off tasks, they just build up until you can't see a way to get through them all. Start viewing the little pockets of time that you have throughout the day as opportunities to accomplish something. Do you have five minutes? Make a phone call or write down a grocery list of items for a new recipe. Do you have ten minutes? Go ahead and pick up the toy room or play a round of Old Maid with the kids. The progress lies in the pockets. Grab a minute here and there and start getting results. Go ahead and fold the laundry when you get it out of the dryer. Put away your jewelry right after you take it off. Don't let the work build up. Keep life manageable by chipping away at it here and there.

When you procrastinate, all you do is waste valuable time that you could be putting toward getting the job done. I am always amazed when one of my children argues for ten minutes about why he or she should not have to do a five-minute task. Why throw away those precious minutes? We all have tasks that we need to do, whether it's weeding a flower bed, mopping a floor, sweating through an exercise video, paying bills, or potty training a child. It's got to be done, so why not just do it now and get it over with? The longer you put it off, the bigger and more daunting the task becomes—and the smaller and less effective your drive and determination become. Don't let life tasks control you. Take control of them by doing them now.

This applies to everything you want to accomplish, the pleasant as well as the unpleasant. Sometimes we even postpone enjoyable activities because of the effort required. But the effort is much larger in our imagination than it is in reality, and the minimum effort always pays you back in huge returns. Whether playing with your kids or romancing your husband, there is no better time than the present. So *do it now*. If you are going to live a healthy, complete, and successful life, then now is the time to take the necessary steps to make it happen. Don't put off living any longer.

Week One, Day Four: Daily Exercises

1. Write the titles Home, Health, Family, and Life in your journal and, underneath these titles, list specific ways that you can apply some action skills to each area. For example, if you have a vision of your family enjoying a meal around the dinner table, then apply some action to it. Do it now by making out a grocery list for tonight's dinner. Build it in blocks by taking fifteen minutes to clear the table of clutter. Make it fun by putting on some music or cutting some flowers for a pretty centerpiece.

2. Now is the time to take action. You should have some type of system to keep everything together—your schedule, your appointment calendar, and those endless lists that every mom keeps. A lot of moms

use PDAs or day planners that can slip into their bags. Personally, I love using a three-ring binder to hold my calendar sheets, grocery lists, and everything else I need to keep track of. My journal is the brain and my planner is the brawn, pushing and pulling my dreams into reality. Today, you need to give yourself the gift of a day planner if you don't already have one. Get a binder and download the Total Mom Planner Sheets from the Web site to stick inside. Now, take some of those actions that you listed in Exercise 1 and write them down on the calendar so you won't let them slip by.

It's a Matter of Attitude

So many people make no effort to control the course of their lives or their emotions. They wake up in either a good mood or a bad mood. They allow good events to make them happy and bad events to get them down. Their emotions are at the whim of whatever life decides to throw at them. You're way ahead of the game. You have decided that life is worth living to the fullest, and you are willing to put forth the effort to make it happen. That is living life on purpose.

Your state of mind is a powerful thing. When you're running on a full tank, you can accomplish anything. When you are strong, confident, and positive, then the world seems to bend to your wishes — not by any magical forces out there somewhere but by the sheer power of your mental and physical state. The opposite is also true. When you find yourself in a weak, depressed, and negative state, then nothing seems to go your way. It's just one big, fat bump in the road after another. On one side, you feel empowered. On the other side, you feel completely powerless. A positive attitude can do wonders for your outlook, but a *power* attitude will enable you to reach your goals. With a power attitude you feel not only positive but also empowered. It's strength, confidence, control, and joy all rolled into one supercharged state of mind.

It's in Your Hands

What a hopeless picture of the world we would have if we thought that everything was out of our control. The truth is, everything boils down to your state of being, and that is something you have complete control over. Let me give you an example. If you are overweight or out of shape, you are most deeply affected by how you *feel* about yourself. If you are having problems in your marriage or with your children, it upsets you most because of how you *feel* about the situation. If your home is a wreck, it's not the home that's bothering you, it's how you *feel* about your home. It's not your money situation that's got you down, but how you *feel* about your money situation. It is not the events that happen in your life that affect your mood, it is how you interpret those events in your mind.

TOTAL MOM TIP
Hourly Attitude Check

Wear a watch that beeps at every hour. This will be your attitude check. Every time it goes off, check your attitude and your actions. Productive actions and a power attitude will enable your vision to become reality. If you pause every hour to focus on developing a power attitude, it will soon become a part of your character.

Power 'Tude

Before you can change your life, you need to realize the power of attitude. Changes in your life don't result in changes in your feelings. It's the opposite. You change your feelings and your outlook, and then you give permission for changes to happen in your life. You're wasting your time if you are waiting for everything to be right in your life before you allow yourself to feel fulfilled and empowered. It will likely never happen. And even in those fleeting moments when it does, the feeling only lasts until you come to the next bump in the road, which is right around the corner. The good life follows the good mind, not the other way around. It's your choice. Let that vision that you have for yourself permeate your mind and empower you. If you want changes to happen in your life, then begin today to live out that vision in your mind and feel empowered because of the direction in which you are headed.

Power Training

I love playing a game with my kids when they are upset about something trivial. I start making jokes with them or doing something silly. Although they vigilantly try to hold on to that frowny face, before long they are laughing and smiling. Their heads are lifted, posture upright, breathing deeper. No matter how hard they try, they cannot get back into that negative state, because a positive one has replaced it. Their circumstances haven't changed, but their perception has been completely altered, and it makes a world of difference. In a nutshell, that's exactly what you need to do to get and keep a power attitude, even when things don't go your way. You push that negativity out with positive energy.

Your emotions and your mind are much more powerful than anything life can throw at you. And if you want to transcend those inevitable bumps in the road and succeed in any area of your life, whether it's your health, home, or family, it all begins with putting yourself into the most productive and powerful state possible.

Six Steps to a Power Attitude

Step One: Recognize the "Bump"

Be conscious of the event or emotion that is threatening to render you powerless. View it in its singularity instead of as a full-blown attack on your mood. For example, if you have a fender bender, don't fall into the mood trap of saying "Everything is going wrong." Instead, see it as

"We have a choice every day regarding the attitude we will embrace for that day. We cannot change our past…we cannot change the fact that people will act in a certain way. We cannot change the inevitable. The only thing we can do is play on the one string we have, and that is our attitude. I am convinced that life is 10% what happens to me and 90% of how I react to it."

—CHARLES SWINDOLL

the singular event that it is—a fender bender. Just by increasing your awareness of the events and emotions to which you respond, you put yourself way ahead of the game.

Step Two: Acknowledge Other Factors

When things go wrong and you feel anger, fear, or despair welling up inside of you, remember to acknowledge other factors that may be affecting your mood. For example, you may be tired or hungry or distracted with other issues. Acknowledge any negative physical or emotional factors so that you can remove them as much as possible from your current situation and channel your energy in a more focused direction.

Step Three: Interrupt the Process

Instead of letting your emotions get caught up in the spiral, interrupt your behavior immediately. The best way to do this is with some type of activity. Go for a walk, sing a song, do a Tarzan yell, anything. Some type of physical action is a great way to draw your focus away from an unwanted thought. You are not ignoring the emotion; you are merely preventing the negative state that will render you powerless to do anything productive about the situation.

Step Four: Get a Powerful Body

Most people don't realize how immensely the body affects the mind. You can't feel energized when you are slumped over with your head down and eyes lowered, nor can you feel depressed when you are standing in a powerful stance with your head lifted, eyes looking upward, taking full, deep breaths. Check your stance, composure, and breathing. When power is exemplified through your body, your brain often takes that as a cue to halt the negative emotions. I see so many moms slumping through life. I want to snatch their elbows off their grocery carts and scream, "It's life! Hold yourself up and get excited!" Yes, even grocery shopping should be done in an energetic, resourceful state. So should making dinner, folding laundry, and playing at the park. It's your life, and you deserve to live it in the most positive state possible.

Step Five: Get a Powerful Mind

Focus on that vision that you have for yourself. Vividly capture that image of who you are becoming with all of your senses. Let all of the good things about your life push out the bad, and channel your mental energy to focus not only on all that you are becoming but also on the progress you have made.

Step Six: Take Action

Redirect your focus by thinking of an effective action you can take to get rid of that bump, find a way over it, or even use it as leverage to gain more success. Replace that bump with something positive, something empowering. Instead of worrying about those bills, sit down and make out a workable budget. Instead of getting angry at your husband, go for a walk and think about everything you love about him. Instead of fretting about your maternal insecurities, make a list of all the ways that you are a good mother. The easiest way to push out the bad is with the good.

RSVP

How do you live by your long-range vision when you are faced with a life of short-term situations? A mom rarely has the luxury of following a plan or progressing logically through her day. She has to jump from washing the breakfast dishes to loading up the car to sweeping up the dirt that her child dumped out of his shoes to cleaning up the milk that spilled all over the kitchen table. Never has there been a career so routine and so unstructured at the same time.

The key to achievement lies in how you respond to the world around you. If you truly believe in the vision that you have set for yourself, your response system will mirror this belief. By your actions, you create your own reality. If you truly believe that you are a healthy person, then you will reach for an apple, a fresh salad, or a slice of whole-grain bread when your stomach starts growling. If you believe that you are a sexy, confident woman, then you will greet your husband with a ten-second kiss instead of a quick little peck.

But sometimes the short-term responses don't go the way you envision them. When you get caught up in the heat of the moment, you end up reacting to a situation rather than responding to it. And believe me, there is a huge difference. Responding requires thought; reacting does not. Responding pushes you forward; reacting pulls you back. Don't let your immediate reactions rob you of the life you want to achieve.

TOTAL MOM TIP
Get to
the Root
of the Issue

Take a look at the Latin root definition of the words *react* and *response*:

React—*Re* (again) + *Act* (to do)
Response—*Re* (again) + *Spondre* (promise)

It's easy to see that one requires more thought than the other. Most of our reactions do indeed turn into do-overs. We regret our actions or our words and wish we had the opportunity to do them again. A response is different. When we establish a vision for ourselves, we believe that the vision will one day be the reality. Our responses become based on that promise. We consider our words and our actions carefully to make sure they reflect that vision. In our responses, we are living for the promise of who we are becoming.

Take a Moment

Most actions that we regret are taken without a moment's hesitation. When life begins closing in on you and you feel the heat rising, it's always best to consciously take a moment to pause and consider before you react to a situation. No matter what the emergency, you can usually afford to take ten seconds to pause and consider what your next move is going to be.

So, let's say that your little boy is in the bathtub and he decides to pour out the entire bottle of shampoo that you picked up from the salon yesterday (which cost you $24). It makes such lovely bubbles that he decides to pick up a cup and pour half of the bathwater onto the floor of the bathroom, and water is now slowly dripping through the subflooring and creating a nice water stain on the kitchen ceiling below. These are the moments when you just want to react. Harsh words can easily come out before you even realize it. And these are also the moments when you need to make a conscious effort to pause and collect yourself before you say or do anything. Things can be repaired, but a broken spirit can stay that way for an awfully long time.

Pausing will allow you to hear the words that you are going to say and see the action you are going to take. It will also give you the opportunity to make sure your words and actions fit with the image of the person you are becoming. Don't be deceived into thinking that the small moments don't matter. Life is nothing more than a series of moments and a chain of responses. Your life is far too valuable and your vision much too deserving to foolishly tear it apart in the heat of the moment. Take a few seconds to pause, and respond in a way that makes you feel proud and complete. You are constantly in the process of creating the person you wish to be, so make every moment count.

Week One, Day Five: Daily Exercises

1. In your journal, write down the four categories that you have been working with—Home, Health, Family, and Life. Under each category, write down some common problem areas in your responses. For example, in the Health category, maybe you eat junk food when you feel stressed. In the Family category, maybe you snap at your husband when you have had a tough day. Now beside each one, write down an effective strategy to handle it and a positive action that can take its place. Think creatively and keep your actions in line with your vision. Instead of eating junk food, stretch up as high as you can, jump up and down, and reach for a healthy snack food, such as a cup of whole-grain cereal or some carrot sticks. Instead of snapping, stand tall, breathe deeply, and go for a warm hug and a deep kiss.

2. Time for some mental rehearsal. Go through the list of positive responses that you just made and visualize yourself doing them. Get the details down and feel the power flowing through you as you do them. By rehearsing them mentally, you will be better prepared to respond positively when the stress-inducing situation occurs.

Weekend Workout

This weekend, you are going to work on establishing an AM and a PM routine to do every single day. These will carry you through the next five weeks (and hopefully the rest of your life). Planning at night and preparing in the morning require only a small time commitment, but you will reap huge rewards.

PM Routine: Set aside a few minutes before you go to bed to prepare your home and everyone in it for the next day. Straighten up the house a bit so that you wake up to a clean slate. Get all of the dishes washed, wipe off the counters, pick up the clutter, and tweak anything else that needs tweaking. Remember, it doesn't need to be perfect, just good enough.

Although you will not begin the exercise portion of this makeover until Week Three, anytime is a great time to make physical activity part of your daily routine. Lay out the clothes and shoes that you are planning to wear the next day. Make sure that everything is comfortable so that you can go on a morning walk or dance with the kids for fifteen minutes.

Now grab your planner before you head to bed and glance through everything you have scheduled for the next day to make sure you are adequately prepared. On Day Four of this week, you listed several actions you can take to reach that vision you have for yourself. Your PM routine is the portion of your day that you will reserve to go over those actions you have planned for the next day. For example, are you running errands tomorrow? Make sure everything you need has been gathered up and put by the door. Do your kids have a game tomorrow? Make sure their uniforms are clean and ready.

AM Routine: This should be the time in which you read your Total Mom Makeover and do the exercises in your journal. This routine is vital because you need to set aside at least twenty minutes in the morning to focus solely on YOU! Make sure you set an alarm to get up and get dressed and ready before anyone else in the house is up. This helps you get a positive perspective on the day and gives you a head start on all that you need to do.

During this time, you need to look over your schedule and any lists you made the night before in your day planner to refresh yourself on the tasks that you need to accomplish. Remember to bring some aspect of play into it as well. This is often the only time a mom can carve out for herself, so enjoy it. Light a scented candle, pour some tea or juice, and sit with an open mind and an open heart. This is also a wonderful time to pray, meditate, or examine some of those goals that you have set. What kind of progress are you making? Is there a different direction you would like to take? What can you do today to live life to its fullest? This is your time to take your dreams and put them into action.

Congratulations!

You made it through Week One! You have made a decision that you want more for your life, and you know the skills you need to develop in order to become the best woman and mother you can be. Now it's time to move on to Week Two and start developing those skills.

BASIC MOM

TOTAL
MOM

CONFIDENT
MOM

NURTURED MOM

SECURE MOM

BASIC MOM

STARTER MOM

Up Your Energy

The Basic Mom has all of her basic needs met in the healthiest and most abundant way possible. You may not be stressing over meeting your needs but you may be living with unnecessary stress because of how you are getting your needs met. Welcome to Basic Mom week, where you start from the beginning to meet your basic needs in the healthiest way possible. You don't just want to survive. You want to thrive! And it begins right now.

Sleep is a basic need. But for moms (especially new moms), sleep is more of a luxury. We never value it more than when we are up three times during the night with a new baby and still have to get up (and stay up) the next morning. If you don't get enough sleep, you feel lethargic, irritable, and disorganized. Even if you are getting enough sleep, you might still have energy dips throughout the day. If you are going to become the best mom you can be, you need to be sure that you have enough energy to accomplish all that you have set out to do. Today you are going to learn how to handle and conquer the energy crisis that is threatening so many moms.

Create a Sanctuary

In order to squeeze in enough sleep, you need to make sure your bedroom is a restful environment. That way, when you do get the rare opportunity to catch some shut-eye, nothing stands in the way. Create a sleep sanctuary by following a few simple guidelines.

- **Remove the television.** We often stay up much later than we should in order to watch television. If getting enough sleep is an issue, then remove the television from your bedroom so that you are not tempted to catch the late, late, late show.

- **Clear out the clutter.** If your bedroom is cluttered, then your mind probably is as well. The most important step here is to make your bed every morning. If you use your bedroom for other purposes, such as a nursery or a home office, then try to keep it as compartmentalized as possible by adjusting dressers or shelves so that one part of the room is spatially separated from the other.

- **Invest in some luxurious linens.** Nothing brings on sleep better than soft, thick, delicious sheets. Buy the highest thread count you can afford (nothing less than 200) and go with a natural fiber, such as cotton or linen.

TOTAL MOM TIP

The Nose Knows

Your sense of smell is extremely powerful, and you can use it to help you wake up or calm down. In my bedroom I use calming scents, such as a lavender-vanilla linen spray. But in the main living areas, especially the kitchen, I use invigorating scents, such as floral- or fruit-scented candles. I also make a natural all-purpose cleaner with water, a squirt of Castile soap, and a few drops of peppermint or lemon essential oil. The scent seems to wake up the entire house.

- ◉ **Create a ritual.** Make a habit of doing something soothing before you go to bed. This serves as a signal to your body to begin shutting down for the night. For example, you may want to read a book in bed every night or have a cup of herbal tea before you turn in.

- ◉ **Use color to your advantage.** Research shows that bright colors, such as red and orange, are stimulating, while blues and greens tend to be more calming. Apply this science to your bedroom by using soothing colors for your walls or linens.

Move Your Body

Lethargy breeds lethargy. When our lifestyles are sedentary, our energy levels sink, and then our lives become even more sedentary. It's a vicious, lazy cycle. Break the cycle by taking ten minutes to get your body moving. This is enough time to jump-start your metabolism and wake up your body and mind.

The tough part of this little trick is getting up and initiating the action. But once you get the ball rolling, it develops a life of its own. Some of the best techniques to get your body moving are dancing to your favorite music or throwing the kids in the stroller and going for a walk (especially if you can meet up with a friend). If you force yourself to get moving when you feel those sleepy waves rolling in, then your body will respond with a big energy boost.

Drink Up!

When you are feeling lethargic, you often reach for something to eat. This is your body's natural response. When energy begins to lag, your body tells your mind that you need to consume calories because food is your source of energy. However, an empty stomach isn't usually the reason we are tired. Our fatigue is probably coming from lack of sleep or is just a result of being sedentary.

Instead of eating, try reaching for a tall glass of ice-cold water. The cold water will wake up your body, and you don't have to worry about burning off the calories. Also, you may be thirsty and not even realize it. Fatigue is usually the first sign of dehydration.

Go Outside

Sometimes we just need to bathe ourselves in sunlight to pick up the pace. If the weather is conducive, then step outside for a few minutes. The change of scenery and the sunshine will help you shake off fatigue. You can even take this one step further by doing something energizing, such as sweeping off the porch or driveway, watering plants, or pulling some weeds. When you go back indoors, you will feel rejuvenated.

PUMP UP THE VOLUME

Music can work wonders. Try some of these booty wigglers to shake off the sleepies:

"Love Shack"—B-52's

"Three Little Birds"—Sean Paul

"Respect"—Aretha Franklin

"What I Like About You"—The Romantics

"Little Miss Can't Be Wrong"—The Spin Doctors

"Real Wild Child"—Everlife

"Good Golly Miss Molly"—Little Richard

"Walkie Talkie Man"—Steriogram

"Can't Stop the World"—The Go-Go's

"Walking on Sunshine"—Aly & AJ

"Can Can"—Bad Manners

"Unwritten"—Natasha Bedingfield

"Dancing with Myself"—Billy Idol

"Greatest Day"—Bowling for Soup

"Release"—Seeed

"One Girl Revolution"—Superchick

Squeeze In a Nap

Sometimes when you feel sleepy the only thing left to do is go to sleep. The problem with naps is that they can leave you feeling groggier than you were before. However, this only happens when the nap lasts too long. The important thing to remember in napping is to try to squeeze in only one sleep cycle. This can usually be accomplished in ten to twenty minutes, and it is enough to replenish your energy. If you go much longer than twenty minutes, your body starts trying to get in a full night's sleep, and waking up just aggravates the situation.

If you begin to feel yourself nodding off but don't want to sleep for too long, then set a wristwatch alarm for about twenty minutes and go ahead and get some rest. When you wake up, you may be tempted to fall back asleep, but try to use some of the other techniques listed to help you wake up and get going.

Don't Dine — Graze

There is a reason why a fiesta is soon followed by a siesta. When you eat a heavy meal, your body has to put a lot of energy toward digesting the food. This leaves you feeling lethargic. If you want to keep a constant level of energy surging through your body all day, then lay off the heavy meals. Instead, try grazing throughout the day. Eating several small meals will help you keep up your energy because your body won't have to work overtime to digest all of the food.

The only big meal I eat during the day is dinner, when the entire family is gathered around the table. The rest of the day I snack. I may have juice for breakfast, an apple an hour later, a handful of cereal about an hour after that. Grazing not only helps you keep up your energy level, it also helps you maintain a healthy weight. You feel constantly satiated, so you won't have the urge to overeat as hunger sets in.

Take Your Vitamins

As your diet improves throughout this makeover, you will notice that your energy levels will increase significantly. The reason for this is that you are removing the foods that cause you to feel lethargic. Healthy foods

"The higher your energy level, the more efficient your body. The more efficient your body, the better you feel and the more you will use your talent to produce outstanding results."
—ANTHONY ROBBINS

can easily be converted to energy without weighing you down. Refined carbs and dense animal protein are particularly prone to slowing down your body.

But every diet can use a little help here and there. B vitamins are essential for a mom because they help the body convert food to energy. People who live with high amounts of stress (bodily and emotional) often need B vitamin supplements to help keep their energy up. And, personally, I cannot think of many more stressful jobs than motherhood. Find a good multivitamin that contains plenty of B vitamins and remember to take it daily.

Breathe In Energy

Breathing is one thing we all do, mostly on a subconscious level. But keep in mind that oxygen is what gives us energy. We breathe in new, vital energy that supplies our bloodstream with oxygen, and when we exhale, we get rid of toxins that have been deposited in our lungs. When we bring our breathing to a conscious level, we can control the depth to which we rid our body of the toxins that are making us feel lethargic and the height to which we energize our bodies. Doing a breathing exercise is a quick and easy way to pour energy into your body when you feel yourself slumping.

Step One: Sit on the floor cross-legged with your palms on the sides of your knees. If that's uncomfortable, then just sit on a chair with your palms on your knees. Make sure your back is straight and your chin up.

Step Two: Breathe in deeply for seven seconds, hold for seven seconds, and then exhale for seven seconds. Repeat this process of deep breathing, being conscious of your chest rising and falling with each breath in and out. Continue for about five complete breaths, feeling your body absorb energy and expel fatigue.

Step Three: This is the part that really energizes. Push down on your knees with your hands and arch your back as you breathe in as deeply as possible. Hold for five to ten seconds, then forcefully exhale that breath as quickly as possible, thoroughly emptying your lungs. Immediately inhale slowly and deeply again, just as before. Hold for five to ten seconds and forcefully exhale again. Repeat this six times. Slowly stand up; you should feel completely cleansed and rejuvenated!

Tune In to Your Biorhythms

You probably already know that everyone has certain biorhythms. You may find that you are more alert in the mornings than in the afternoons. My husband, Blair, and I are completely different when it comes to biorhythms. When the alarm goes off in the morning, I jump out of bed, throw on my exercise clothes, juice some carrots, sing some songs, and dance in the kitchen. It takes Blair about ten minutes to get out of bed and make it to the sofa, where he sits for another fifteen. After that he shuffles into the kitchen and pours his coffee. By the second cup he usually manages to open his eyes.

Your biorhythms are distinctly yours, so use them to your advantage. I often hear experts say that you should schedule your high-activity tasks when you are most alert and your low-activity tasks when you are less alert. This doesn't work for me (nor for any mom I know). If I scheduled my low-activity tasks, such as writing or paying bills, when I was least alert, I would just zonk out right there at my desk. The opposite actually works better for moms. Schedule your low-activity tasks when you are wide awake so you don't have to worry about propping your eyes open with toothpicks. And when the energy begins to wane, you need to force yourself to do high-activity tasks, such as gardening or vacuuming, because these activities will help boost your energy.

Week Two, Day One: Daily Exercises

1. In your journal, write down the things in your life that may be dragging your energy down. For example, you may have an infant who needs to nurse frequently during the night, or you may have to work late hours. You may be low on energy because of other factors such as high stress, a poor diet (that is changing), a sedentary lifestyle (that is going to change, too), or just that mysterious midafternoon slump. Write these things down and, beside each, write one of today's tips that you can employ to boost your energy. For sleep that is disrupted by a nursing baby, create a nice, calming bedroom and try to turn in a few hours earlier. For a sedentary lifestyle, you may want to put on some music and get your body moving every few hours. For that midafternoon slump, try the breathing exercise instead of pouring a cup of coffee. Find some solutions and start using them.

2. Take some time today to straighten up your bedroom. Get rid of any clutter that's lying around, change the sheets if they need it, and vacuum the floor. You can also make a pleasant linen spray by putting a few drops of fabric softener into a spray bottle of water and adding a favorite essential oil. Shake it up and spray it on your sheets before you climb in.

3. Practice Action Skill #7: Do It Now. This week, make your bed as soon as you wake up. This small step will encourage you to maintain a pleasant environment in your bedroom. It's so much more relaxing to turn down a bed at night instead of crawling into a messy one.

Sensational Sex

It may not seem like it at times, especially when the baby keeps you up until 3:00 AM, but sex is a basic need that all of us have. Unfortunately, moms live such a crazy life that this very basic need often gets neglected. After a full day of sweeping up Cheerios, changing diapers, trucking back and forth to the soccer field, scrubbing toilets, and trying to squeeze back into your prepregnancy jeans, the last thing you want to do is don a feathered negligee and do a little striptease for your husband.

But sex is a lot like exercise. We all love what it does to our bodies, but sometimes it's hard to get the ball rolling. Sex is meant to be enjoyed and celebrated. It makes you feel youthful and attractive. It can clear your mind, energize your body, and even build up your resistance to disease. Not only do you *need* to have this pleasure in your life, but you also *deserve* it. A healthy sex life will enrich your marriage, your health, your life, and even your mothering (a satisfied mommy is a happy mommy).

So if you have been denying yourself the pleasure and benefits of healthy sex, it's time to change that. Unfortunately, it's not always easy for moms. We have three primary obstacles that stand in our way: lack of opportunity, lack of drive, and lack of confidence. Work through these areas, and your sex-kitten days are back.

Lack of Opportunity

It was so much easier before the kids came along. You didn't have to worry about barricading your door or muffling the screams of pleasure. But here you are with little ears, little eyes, and little bodies running and crawling through the house. Although the days of groping each other on the staircase or slamming down on the kitchen counter may be temporarily behind you (there are always babysitters and summer camp), you can still carve out special times to enjoy intimacy.

- **Sex on the Fly:** There is nothing like a quickie in the closet to release tension and to make your husband thank the sex gods that you married him. You can even surprise him by slipping off your panties underneath your skirt, making sure the kids are happy and occupied, and then telling him you need him to check out a leak in the bathroom. After you get him cornered, lock the door and attack.

- **Date Night:** You and your husband should enjoy regular evenings together. Even if you don't get all dolled up and go out dancing, you can still turn off the TV, break open a bottle of champagne, and enjoy each other after the kids have gone to bed. If you do get the opportunity to go out on a date, throw in some spice by kissing and touching him before you even get out of the car at the restaurant (during dinner, you'll be thinking about getting a piece of chocolate cake for dessert; he'll be thinking about getting a piece of something else).

- **Turndown Service:** Don't let sleep sneak up on you! Take as many measures as possible to ensure that the two of you are going to bed at the same time, with books closed and the television off. Leave the ratty old T-shirts for craft projects. Wear something sexy to bed or, better yet, nothing at all. Your husband will love the surprise of climbing into bed and finding your naked body waiting there for him.

⊚ **Wake-up Service:** Here is another opportunity that many of us fail to take advantage of. Okay, morning breath may be an issue, but your body will feel so good within a few minutes of lovemaking that you won't care if he licked the toilet beforehand. And don't forget about those still moments in the middle of the night when you wake up to get a drink of water or settle a child down into bed. Wake up your husband for some quiet sex.

The important thing about finding opportunities for intimacy is to get your priorities straight. Watching television or getting caught up with your scrapbooking may be easier, but it is not going to build a happy and healthy marriage. Seek moments throughout the day and night to be intimate with your husband.

"Sex is one of the nine reasons for reincarnation... The other eight are unimportant."
—HENRY MILLER

You don't need to place a bulk order through an online sex shop. Some of the best sex toys are already in your home: ⊚ **Paintbrushes**—You don't need to be an artist to test your creative ability. Try getting him aroused by slowly stroking his naked body with a paintbrush. ⊚ **Ice**—Slide it over his body or yours. ⊚ **Oranges**—Bring some slices to bed. Squeeze the juice over his body or yours and take turns licking it off. ⊚ **Scarves**—You do not want your kids asking you why there are handcuffs hanging from the headboard. If you would like to play around with bondage, go soft. ⊚ **Plastic wrap**—It's not just for casseroles. Try wrapping yourself up and letting him peel it away. ⊚ **Whipped cream**—Yeah, it's trite. But it's still fun! Squirt it on your body and his and enjoy the dessert.

Caution: Do not use any of these internally.

TOTAL MOM TIP
**The Power
of Play**

Lack of Drive

Even when we do have the opportunity, lack of drive is something that all moms struggle with at one time or another. It's perfectly normal. We all have those occasional dry spells. As a matter of fact, more than half of women suffer from loss of libido at some time in their lives. Keep this in mind and be patient with yourself. Phases come and go, but there are some effective ways to help the slump pass.

◉ **Focus:** As a mom, you probably have a million things running through your head. This is good when you are trying to make dinner, entertain a toddler, and talk on the phone at the same time. But this is not good when the lights are turned down low and Barry White is crooning in the background. Achieving and maintaining your focus is a vital part of your sex drive.

Try to clear your thoughts of the house, the errands, the kids, and everything else swimming around in your head, and focus on the touching, the breathing, the feeling of your bodies against each other. If it helps, imagine that you are making love in a special place, such as on a beach, in an elevator, even on a stage. When you catch your mind wandering, make a conscious effort to tune in to a physically pleasing aspect of lovemaking.

◉ **Communicate:** If you are feeling a loss of drive, then you need to make sure you are communicating this to your husband. Let him know that you are struggling and reassure him that it is in no way a reflection on him (unless, of course, it is; then you definitely need to discuss that issue).

Another important thing you need to communicate is what you want out of sex. If you don't voice your desires, then you may as well be playing blindman's bluff. Let your husband know how and where you want to be touched, the positions you enjoy, or even some secret fantasies, such as a shared bubble bath or making love in the backseat of the car (or minivan). If you don't feel comfortable talking about your desires, then begin with nonverbal communication. Place your hands over his and guide them over your body, or initiate new positions.

⊚ **Break the Monotony:** Change is good, especially where sex is concerned. One reason that our libido wanes over time is that our sex life simply becomes boring—same place, same time, same position. Sprinkle some spice into the mix every now and then. A fresh take on lovemaking will put a sparkle in your eye and a spring in your step.

Be careful about revealing your sex fantasies to your husband. Some are certainly safe enough, such as new places and positions. But test the waters before you bring out the bike chains or ask him to dress up like Colonel Sanders. He may think you have had a meltdown. And some fantasies are best kept to yourself (you don't want to get caught screaming, "Oh, Brad Pitt!" during an orgasm).

TOTAL MOM TIP
Strip It Down
and
Sex It Up

Indulging in your sex fantasies is a great way to spice up a boring bedroom. After the kids have gone to bed, don some of your sexiest lingerie under your clothes and do a striptease for your husband (music and everything). But make sure the bedroom door is locked—walking in on a stripper mom could take years of therapy to get over!

If you feel uncomfortable or are unsure of what to do, there are some awesome video exercise programs (yes, stripping can be a cardio workout). Jeff Costa and Carmen Electra both have great videos. Many exercise facilities are also offering strip classes. Of course, you don't actually strip down to nothing, but you will get a good workout and learn some awesome moves to try out on your husband. The shyness factor usually disappears after the first few minutes, so go ahead and try it out.

In order to try out new terrain, hint around it when you're not in bed. For example, you may want to mention that you were reading about how men love it when their partners talk dirty to them. Ask his opinion. If he is appalled, then go ahead and keep it quiet. But if he seems intrigued, then work on some key phrases to throw around during sex.

Lack of Confidence

A mom's self-esteem is a precious thing indeed. One day you are strutting your hot little self along the path of life. You pause for a moment to have a baby, or two, or seven. The next thing you know you have boobs that could catch a strong wind and fly away and pounds of postpartum flab hanging off your abs. Confidence is a difficult thing to muster when your body looks better under the sheets than on top of them. But before you turn out all of the lights during lovemaking, there are a few secrets you should know.

Secret #1: You Care More Than He Does

It's true. Your husband probably doesn't care nearly as much as you do that your breasts may have lost some of their perkiness or that you have a little more cushion on your tush. He cares about one thing — sex. He is attracted to the unity that the two of you share. When it comes to appearance, you are your worst critic. For some reason, we expect our lovemaking episodes to resemble the cover of a Harlequin novel, with our voluptuous breasts saluting our lover and our svelte thighs wrapped around his waist. Our bodies will never be perfect, but they can always be passionate. Forget about pulling the sheets up to your chin. The bedroom is no place for shame or inhibition. You care a lot more about your physical imperfections than your husband does, so ease up a bit and allow yourself to enjoy the experience. Just once, go for some no-

LOOK GOOD NAKED

If body image is a problem, there are some sneaky ways to look better naked. Try some of these to build up your confidence:

Sunless tanning lotion—Follow the directions and apply this all over your body. It helps hide cellulite and gives your naked body a warm, inviting glow.

Manicures and pedicures—Keep your nails looking pretty. Even beautiful painted nails are like jewelry on your naked body.

Tousled hair—Women usually look pretty good after a roll in the hay. Get his blood pumping by looking like you've already been warming up.

Skin shimmer—There are a lot of shimmering lotions on the market. They help hide imperfections while giving your body a shimmery, seductive appeal.

Makeup—There is a reason they are called bedroom eyes. Play up the eyes with liner and mascara, then use a nude gloss on the lips.

Aroma—A sultry scent heightens the sexual experience. Don't go too heavy, but lightly apply an inviting perfume that will whet his appetite.

Hairy issue—Some guys may like it bushy but experiment with getting a bikini wax, a Brazilian, or just shaving yourself down to nothing. See what turns him on. You can also get permanent laser hair removal and never worry about the upkeep.

holds-barred, back-scratching, whoopin'-it-up sex and see his reaction. I guarantee he won't be complaining about any excess jiggle.

Secret #2: It's All About Attitude

The physical side of sex is great. But physical sex is a combination of several factors—genital stimulation, verbal and visual cues, and, most important, attitude. Sexual prowess does not come from appearance. It comes from confidence. Make a conscious effort to hold a kiss longer and deeper, caress him when he least expects it, and try out some new moves. Don't just be on the receiving end. Instead, give him something that stays in his mind for days afterward.

If you still feel uncomfortable about your body, then start taking small steps to open up a bit more. Instead of groping in the dark, go for low lighting, such as candles or a string of decorative lights. Instead of white cotton panties, wear a lace bikini or thong. Little steps like these will help build up your confidence, and his responses will encourage you to take it a few steps further. Sex isn't always pretty, but it can always be beautiful. Get over your body image and start enjoying yourself. And do not neglect this very important part of your life.

Week Two, Day Two: Daily Exercises

1. In your journal, make a list of everything you love about your husband. Try to look past the grudges you may be holding or the negative qualities he may have, and search out those traits that first attracted you to him. By focusing on the positive, you can lay the groundwork for sensational sex.

2. Spice up your lovemaking by adding a creative touch here and there. Do a striptease for him, buy some sexy lingerie, step into the shower with him, or bring a bowl of sliced oranges to bed. You can even surprise him by hiring a sitter and spending the night at a hotel.

3. Practice Action Skill #3: Have Fun. Find one unavoidable task that you don't enjoy, such as washing the car or cleaning the bathrooms. Now think creatively and come up with a way you can make it more fun and try it out. Perhaps you and the kids can play with the hose while all of you wash the car, or you can clean the bathroom while a child is in the tub so you can accomplish the task while you enjoy spending time with her. You can even apply this skill to your sex life if you are suffering through a particularly bad dry spell. Is there a fantasy you would like to play out with your husband? Go ahead — practice some boldness and try it out.

Cut the Clutter

"Have nothing in your houses that you do not know to be useful or believe to be beautiful."
—WILLIAM MORRIS

You probably don't have to worry about whether or not you have a roof over your head. But how you care for your home makes a huge difference in your life. It affects your health, your spirit, and your entire outlook. And when you surround yourself with clutter and mess, it eventually begins to invade your personal life. In order to maximize your abilities and reach your potential, you need to begin with a clean and clear slate. And that starts in your home.

If I were to tell you why some of us have a tendency to clutter up our homes and how we can get rid of the mess, this part of the book would have to be about 150 pages long. But today I simply want to show you how much time and energy we waste on maintaining clutter and get you motivated to clear it out. Clutter is toxic. It can zap your energy and your peace of mind in one fell swoop. So roll up those sleeves and let's get started.

The Clutter Questions

Many of us are guilty of devoting too many of our precious resources to the care and keeping of clutter. You can waste resources on useless things like clutter, or you can use them to reach your goals and be the best mom you can be. Before you let another day go by with stacks of papers on the counters and piles of clothes stuffed in your closets, ask yourself a few questions:

Do you have the time for clutter? Have you ever been stuck on your way out of the house searching for your keys, your purse, your shoes, or, worse, your kids' shoes? According to the American Demographic Society, Americans spend more than nine million hours a day searching for lost and misplaced items. Clutter consumes so much time because it not only hides things we need but also takes time to collect, move, and clean. Don't throw precious time away by playing hide-and-seek with your clutter (kids, yes; clutter, no).

**TOTAL MOM TIP
Makeover
Magic**

If you need some serious incentive to get rid of clutter, then do a room makeover. But here's the catch—use only the money you get from selling the clutter you collect (or from the deduction you can take). With a clear image in your mind of what you are going for, you are more likely to be able to part with the clutter. I recently collected a bunch of old clothes and shoes, donated them to a charity, tallied up the amount that I could deduct from my taxes, and then went out and spent that amount on a closet makeover—new closet organizers, some pretty baskets, and matching hangers. I even had enough left over to buy a new pair of shoes.

Do you have the money for clutter? We pay not only to collect our clutter, but also to keep it. You pay to heat, cool, and maintain every square foot of your home, and that includes the square footage that is being used to house clutter. Make clutter earn its keep. If you have a piece of furniture, make sure you are using it effectively. If you have a lot of clothes, make sure you are wearing them. You also pay to collect and maintain that clutter in other ways. How much money do you pay for that boat that you only use two to three times a year? What about that exercise machine that just gathers dust in the corner? If you are not using it, get rid of it. You can make money by selling the clutter or by donating it and writing off the deduction.

Do you have the room for clutter? Clutter takes up so much valuable space in our homes. Just think about what you could do with all of that room — create an art studio, a tearoom, a reading nook, a teen hangout. The possibilities are endless. Clutter contaminates our environment and robs us of breathing room. You and your family deserve a home that is enriching and nurturing, and that happens when everything in it fulfills a distinct purpose.

Do you have the energy for clutter? We spend a large amount of time taking care of clutter, more than you might realize. I have a good friend who comes over once every two weeks to dust, vacuum, and shine up my house. She only works for two hours, but my family and I need to work for at least four hours just to prepare for her arrival. We need to get the laundry out of the way, pick up the toys, clean under the beds, get the trash out of the house, move everything off the counters and desks, and take care of other things that result from clutter. It's amazing how much housework is just picking up, putting away, and shuffling back and forth. And it's amazing, too, how easy housework would be if the clutter were eliminated.

Do you have the attitude for clutter? By far, the most important reason to cut down on the clutter is this: Clutter robs us of peace of mind. There's just something about order and simplicity that calms our spirits. Clutter can be like nails on a chalkboard, creating unnecessary tension and frustration for us. Your home should lift you up, not drag you down. Every moment you invest in eliminating clutter is a moment that you invest in your emotional well-being. You deserve a life that is clutter free!

You didn't bring all of the clutter into your home by yourself, so don't think you have to get rid of it by yourself. Get your family to help out. Teach your children philanthropy at a young age by getting them to collect items for donations. For example, if they have a drawer full of clothes, you can advise them to pull out any clothes that they no longer enjoy wearing and put them in a bag for someone else. If they have a difficult time with this project, then you may need to set clearer parameters such as "Find five shirts you can give away" or the opposite, "Find five shirts you want to keep." But remember that you are not in this alone. Let your children help out with the de-cluttering, and they'll learn some valuable life lessons in the process.

TOTAL MOM TIP
Clutter-free Kids

Plan of Attack

If you need to de-clutter your house, then make sure you do it right. If you dive in head first without a clear plan of attack, you are probably going to be left with a bigger mess than the one you started with.

◎ **Collect your tools.** You will need four containers—one for trash (trash bags work well), a second for donations (cardboard boxes or sturdy paper bags), a third for "put away" items (a laundry basket is perfect), and a fourth for "I can't part with it yet" items (a plastic or cardboard box).

◎ **Select one project at a time.** Don't just start grabbing at stuff. Select the one area you will work on, such as a closet or drawer, and make sure you have adequate time to complete it. I know distractions are inevitable, especially with little ones around, but try to zero in on your target and keep working at it until you're finished.

- ◉ **Don't handle something more than once.** This is a trick that works wonders. Sometimes when we are trying to clear out clutter we pick up objects, handle them for a while without knowing what to do with them, and then put them back down, only to pick them up again and repeat the process. When you pick something up, put it in one of the containers with no rest stops in between.

- ◉ **Put everything where it belongs.** Put the trash in the outdoor trash can. Put the donation box in your car to drop off at the center. Put the items that belong somewhere in the house in their proper places. And if there are any items that you feel you just can't part with, box them up, label the box, and stick it in your attic, garage, or somewhere out of the way. Now put a note on the calendar four months from that date to go back to the items in the box. If you have been fine that long without them, you don't need them — try to make yourself sell them or give them away.

- ◉ **Reward yourself.** Give yourself a treat for a job well done. When you finish de-cluttering, pour a cup of tea, polish your nails, munch on a cookie, watch a favorite movie, or do something that you especially love. Eliminating clutter is hard work, and you should reward your efforts.

- ◉ **Keep the cycle going.** "Clutter in, clutter out." This will be your new mantra. Repeat it until it rolls off your tongue with ease and grace. Clutter is inevitable. We are always going to have junk appearing in the nooks and crannies of our homes and multiplying in its quiet little corners. So don't think for a minute that your cleaned-out garage will stay that way. Clutter is sneaky. It's mischievous. It will find ways to creep in without your consent.

So let the march continue. Let the clutter come in, and then march it right back out again. At our house, we make getting rid of clutter a constant endeavor. There is always a bag or box at the ready to deposit anything that needs to go to the donation center. When someone grows out of an article of clothing and it's not being passed down, it goes in the box. When I am picking up toys and notice some that the kids no longer play with, these go in the box. When I bring home new linens, the old ones go in the box. Once a month (sometimes more often), we drop off a load at the donation center. It's a clutter cycle. Just make sure that you keep the cycle going.

Week Two, Day Three: Daily Exercises

1. In your journal, divide your home into zones. Try not to go over six zones, or it will become too much to keep up with. I divided my home into five zones: Zone 1—kitchen, dining room, pantry; Zone 2—living room, breakfast room, office; Zone 3—bathrooms; Zone 4—kids' bedrooms; Zone 5—master bedroom. Give yourself one zone a week in which to do some serious de-cluttering. Remind yourself by writing the zone on a calendar with a big number on each Monday, and post a little chart next to it that lists your zones. It may feel a bit regimented, but it is an easy plan that will help you make a lot of progress. After you finish all the zones, the cycle begins again.

2. Use today, tomorrow, or the weekend to begin de-cluttering your first zone. And remember to reward yourself with something extra special.

3. Practice Action Skill #5: Build It in Blocks. When you begin tackling that first zone, practice some of the block party tips, such as the Ten-Minute Tidy, where you only de-clutter for ten minutes and then take a break. You can also get the family involved. Maybe you can all watch a movie together after the zone is de-cluttered. You'll be surprised at how quickly you can get the zone de-cluttered if everyone works for ten minutes straight or does a Clean Up Countdown.

Dump the Frump

O kay, so your basic need of clothing is met. Or at least I hope so. I would hate to think that you are running around naked somewhere. But *how* is it being met? Are you throwing on the same baggy clothes or shapeless T-shirts every morning? Or do you take a few extra minutes to look good? No matter how much emphasis we put on inner beauty, appearance truly does matter — to the world, to your family, and, most deeply, to you.

You Don't Need a Paycheck

We all have a tendency to value things that we associate with money. If the bag that you picked up from Target gets dirt on it, you don't care. But if you get dirt on your Louis Vuitton, then you're likely to fly into hysterics. The same logic applies to our careers.

We often have a tendency to devalue our jobs as mothers and homemakers because there is no paycheck associated with them. We wear our emotions on our sleeve, quite literally — especially when that sleeve has a torn hem and a big spit-up stain on it. The truth is, we dress the part. If you take a great amount of pride in your career as a home manager, then it will show in your appearance. And if you are still buying into the ridiculous idea that you are "*just* a mom," then that disparaging philosophy will also manifest itself through your appearance.

When we have paying careers, we tend to respect ourselves more. We get up early enough to get dressed and look nice. We do our hair and our makeup. We wear shoes that coordinate with our bags. But something happens when we choose to make motherhood our full-time profession. We skip a shower (or two). We wear those pants that are a bit *too* comfortable (I once heard a woman refer to her frumpy pants as "lounge britches"). We forget to style our hair or put on mascara. Slowly but surely, we begin asking the eternal question, What's the point?

Well, I have five.

TOTAL MOM TIP
**Time on
Your Side**

You can no longer use the excuse that you don't have time to get yourself ready. Cosmetics companies understand that time is extremely limited for women, and they are constantly coming out with new time-saving products. You can buy two-in-one lotion and tanner, disposable makeup-remover wipes, two-in-one shampoo and conditioner, long-wearing lipstick and eyeliner, tinted moisturizers, and much more. Try some of these products and streamline your beauty routine.

Point #1: Your Self-Esteem

People often show how they feel about themselves through their appearance. When you frump around looking like something the dog dragged in, you show that you don't have a great amount of respect for yourself. Sure, there are days when you only leave the house to take out the trash, but appearance and self-esteem go hand in hand. When you look good, you feel good.

You are doing wonderful work. Even if you never earn another penny in your life, you are contributing more to your world by simply being there for your family. Take pride in your life choices and show it in your appearance! Being a mom does not need to be a self-sacrificial way of living, and no one is doling out points to the mom who looks the most pathetic and altruistic. You can give your all to your family without giving up your sense of style.

Point #2: Your Children

It is not just the mirror that reflects your image. Being a mother means that you are under the constant scrutiny of little eyes absorbing every bit of you. It is an awe-inspiring feeling, knowing that every good thing about you — and every bad thing that you try to keep hidden — is exposed to the ones you love and care for most deeply. It's a feeling like no other, and it will compel you to be the best mother, and the greatest woman, you can possibly be. In everything you do, you are teaching and your children are learning. What are they learning about how much you respect your career as a mother and a homemaker? I want my children to see that motherhood is a beautiful and challenging career, and not something to consider lightly. Your children need to see that you put just as much thought, energy, and preparation into this career as you would into any other profession. And much of that message is unspoken. It is communicated in your appearance and your attitude. What are you telling them every single day?

Point #3: Your Husband

It's not just you and your children who are at a disadvantage when you don't put any effort into your appearance. Your husband gets the short end of the stick, too. As shallow as it may seem, it's not always the inner beauty that gets your husband's engine running. Keep the flame burning by giving him something pleasing to feast his eyes upon. If he

FIVE MUST-HAVES IN THE TOTAL MOM CLOSET

Once you have the basic ingredients of a great wardrobe, all you need to do is accessorize your outfit and get on with the day. Stock your wardrobe with these basic essentials in order to streamline your routine:

1. **SHOES**—Make sure your shoes are casual enough to be comfortable but stylish enough to show that you have some fashion sense.

2. **JEANS**—Ditch the mom jeans and get a trendy cut that shows off your figure. If you need to, shop with a friend who can help you pick out a stylish pair.

3. **SKIRTS**—Yes, moms are allowed to wear cute skirts. Choose styles that are casual enough to move in, and don't be scared to show a little leg.

4. **TOPS**—Forget about the baggy T-shirts and choose some flirty tops or some fitted tees. You don't want to look like you are living in your pajamas.

5. **JACKETS**—A casual fitted jacket does wonders to pull an outfit together. You can wear trendy jackets with skirts, tees, jeans, and everything in between.

is the primary breadwinner, then send him off with an attractive image to keep in his mind throughout the workday (not you running around in a housecoat and slippers). And when he comes home at the end of the day, don't let a frustrated, harried, disheveled woman greet him. It will mean getting up a few minutes earlier or spending a little extra time in the bathroom in the afternoon, but it is so worth it.

It's not sexist to want to look good for your husband. It's considerate. I would slowly but surely lose respect for my husband if he lounged around in old pajama pants, unshaven and stinky. We both work from home, so there is definitely the temptation to just "let ourselves go." But we both get up early to shower and dress, not just for our jobs but for each other. We are professionals in our business, as well as sensual in our marriage. Who wants to snuggle with a frump? Putting some effort into your appearance will not only give you a confidence boost but also make your husband proud, happy, and more stimulated than a six-pack of Red Bull!

Point #4: Your Career

Being a mom isn't just a full-time profession. It is the most challenging full-time profession you could ever have. It requires every bit of your skill and energy, so keep this in mind when it is time to get ready in the mornings. Get up early and dress for success. Frumping out not only makes it look as if you are a slacker at your job but also shows the world that you do not deserve respect for your career choice. For yourself, the world, and moms everywhere, dump the frump and start projecting a professional image.

Point #5: Your Motivation

It's so true: When you look good, you feel good. When you feel good, you get more done. When you get more done, you feel even better. This is a cycle you definitely want to get caught up in! Now think about the other side of the coin. When you look bad, you feel bad. When you feel bad, you are not motivated to do anything. When you don't get anything done, you feel even worse. It's a no-brainer. The first option is, by far, the best. Anything that you can do to get yourself motivated is a worthwhile investment.

Boosting your appearance will definitely boost your motivation and heaven knows, moms can use all the motivation they can get. Dressing well from head to toe puts you in top form for the day ahead. Even on those inevitable days when you can't dig deep enough to find the motivation, getting fully and stylishly dressed will help you get into character. Just see your career as a Hollywood movie. You may not feel

"I don't understand how a woman can leave the house without fixing herself up a little—If only out of politeness. And then, you never know, maybe that's the day she has a date with destiny. And it's best to be as pretty as possible for destiny."

—COCO CHANEL

like playing a role, but you still get into wardrobe, style your hair, and do your makeup. And after all that is over, you find, much to your surprise, that you have actually become the character. Sometimes in motherhood you need to "fake it until you make it."

Many moms don't wear shoes in their homes, but I am a die-hard shoe fan. For some reason, this one simple act can set the tone for the entire day. You are in performance mode and ready for anything! I guarantee that if Fortune 500 companies instituted a "no shoe policy," productivity would decrease significantly. Get the production curve working in your favor by slipping on some shoes.

Girl Power

What a great time to be a woman. We don't just look powerful we *are* powerful! We don't have to dress like men to be the president of a corporation and we don't have to wear robes and slippers to be stay-at-home moms. Being a full-time mom requires quick thinking, sharp skills, incredible endurance, and power. And dressing feminine, once considered a sign of weakness, is now considered a sign of strength. Forget the man suits with the shoulder pads. Girl power can be spaghetti straps, ruffles, boots, stilettos, blue jeans, a mini, or anything else that we pick from our closets. But whatever it is, there is no denying that beauty is strength.

Taking time to look good is empowering. It's a way to get going and feel strong while you're at it. Every challenging occupation has its uniform. A soldier has camouflage. A scuba diver has a wet suit. And a mom needs to put on what I affectionately refer to as her "butt-kickin" boots. This doesn't mean you're going to kick someone's butt. This means you are going to kick the butt of everything that stands in the way of doing a superlative job. You are kicking out laziness. You are kicking out negativity. You are kicking everything out of your way, and you are going forward, full steam ahead. You don't have the time or the energy to feel afraid or ashamed. You've got better things to do, and you've got the boots to make those things happen.

Week Two, Day Four: Daily Exercises

1. Grab your journal and head to your closet. Go through your wardrobe and make a pile of all those clothes that don't make you feel attractive and energized. If you have something you are emotionally attached to but it doesn't meet this criteria, pull it out of your closet and stick it in a box to pack up and put away. You don't want anything in your closet that doesn't work (this includes your shoes). Now write down in your journal some key pieces that you may need to add to your wardrobe. For example, every mom needs a good pair of sexy jeans, some khakis, some fitted cotton tops, attractive shoes, and a few pretty jackets to throw on top. Sell the clothes you are getting rid of and use the money to buy these pieces, or donate them and use the tax refund.

2. When you do your PM routine and set out your outfit for the next day, remember to add some jewelry to go with it. This little step will set the tone not only for your appearance but for your entire day. When you are wearing nice jewelry, it's practically impossible to frump out.

3. Practice Action Skill #4: Be Selective. Clean the bathrooms in your home before you go to bed. But here's the trick: Just clean until it "looks" clean. Wipe off the mirror and counters, swish the scrubber around the toilet, spray cleaner on the floor, throw a rag on the ground and "mop" the floor with your foot. You will look so much more attractive in a clean mirror!

Extreme Diet Makeover

Food is definitely a basic need. You can't survive too long without it. Hopefully, you don't have to worry too much about meeting your basic need to eat, but the food that most moms consume is holding them back from becoming all that they could be. Poor nutrition equals poor health, and there is just no way around it. As a mom, you need and deserve lasting energy so that you can keep up with your kids and the demands of your lifestyle. And the only way to get that lasting energy is to fuel your body for performance.

If you are reluctant to make changes in your diet, keep in mind that this is the one step that has the highest return on your investment. Eating a healthy diet will give you more energy to get everything on your to-do list accomplished. It will alter your mood significantly, making you feel happier and more optimistic. It will also improve your physical appearance. You will have a brighter and clearer complexion, shiny hair, strong nails, and a healthy and stable weight. Your kids will also benefit from a healthy diet, and you will be spending a lot less time in the pediatrician's office!

Slow and Steady

Real and lasting changes don't usually happen overnight. Instead, they often result from small steps taken along the way. This diet makeover may seem a bit daunting at first, but I want to encourage you to take it one step at a time. Make adjustments every day, and you will find that those incremental steps will lead you to a healthier body and mind. You will begin the diet makeover today, but you will carry through the weekend and next week in order to build real and lasting changes. So don't set fire to your pantry or dump the contents of your fridge into the trash. Huge overhauls can often backfire on you. The Total Mom Diet is vastly different from the standard American diet, so give yourself time, patience, and a little leniency along the way.

This diet will be a much bigger change for some moms than for others, so start where you are. If you are accustomed to drinking seven sodas a day, just cut back one soda a day over a week or so. If you only eat white bread, just replace your sandwich bread one week, your buns and rolls the next, and so on, until you are consuming predominantly

TOTAL MOM TIP
The Price
Is Right

When you first begin looking for healthier alternatives to poor nutrition, you may get a dose of sticker shock. Soy milk costs more than dairy milk. Date sugar costs more than white sugar. Organic costs more than nonorganic. And so the story goes, on down the receipt. Try cost-saving techniques such as purchasing items in bulk. If you get to know the manager of your local health food store, you may even be allowed to purchase large amounts of food at wholesale cost. And remember how much money you are saving on junk food, medical bills, and medications. You may be spending a bit more, but you can't put a price tag on feeling great and getting the most out of life.

whole grains. Your actions can take place over a course of days, weeks, or months. This diet makeover is meant to start the ball rolling to a healthier and happier you.

Cut Out the B.A.D. C.R.A.P.!

There are seven main food culprits that may be robbing you of good health. These seven foods are also prevalent in the standard American diet: **B**ad fats, **A**ddictive substances, **D**airy, **C**hemicals, **R**efined carbohydrates, **A**nimal protein, and **P**rocessed foods, and all together they spell BAD CRAP! By cutting them out of your diet, you will be well on your way to a brand-new body and life.

B is for Bad Fat. Even if you don't have a problem squeezing into your jeans, you may have a problem with fatty deposits squeezing through your bloodstream. That's the tricky thing about fat. Research shows that the total *amount* of fat in a diet, whether high or low, isn't really linked to disease. What really matters is the *type* of fat. And there is good fat and bad fat.

TOTAL MOM TIP
Sneaky Fat

Choose healthy baked foods instead of going deep-fried. Use olive oil, canola oil, and margarine with no trans fat. Remember to read all labels carefully because that fat can be sneaky.

Good fats are a very important part of your diet. They reduce harmful cholesterol; cushion, insulate, and lubricate organs; and aid in metabolism. You can recognize foods with good fats because they are usually labeled monounsaturated or polyunsaturated, or they tout the label "zero trans fat." Some examples of good fats are olive oil, canola oil, nuts, and avocados. Bad fats, which are usually labeled as saturated or trans fat, are difficult to process and eventually end up getting stored in your body (in sweet little spots like your arteries, your thighs, and that flabby area under your upper arm). Bad fats can be found in margarines, shortenings, and anything deep-fried. Try to avoid foods that include saturated, hydrogenated, or partially hydrogenated fat. Most commercial fast foods, baked goods, and fried foods use saturated fats, so read labels carefully and know what you are putting into your mouth (and your bloodstream).

A is for Addictive Substances. Okay, I enjoy a good macchiato as much as the next mom, but most people consume way too many addictive substances. If you smoke or drink excessive alcohol, cut it out of your life. If you can't, seek professional help in this area. But addictive substances can also sneak in the back door, and before you know it, your health is being held hostage.

Caffeine and sugar can be very addictive—so much so that you can feel pretty horrible when you try to go without them. And we all know that if you have a little, it usually just whets your appetite for more. The rule of thumb for any addictive substance is this: If you find that you need it more than you want it, then it's time to do without it. Your health is far too valuable and your family too important for you to play around with anything that can create a dependency.

TOTAL MOM TIP
Be a Weaner

According to the *American Journal of Clinical Nutrition,* anything over three eight-ounce cups of coffee a day is considered unhealthy. But play it safe and keep it around two or less. If you are weaning yourself off coffee or significantly decreasing the amount that you consume, then plan for at least three to four days to make the transition. If this is especially difficult, you can substitute green tea and slowly taper that down.

D is for Dairy.—Are you ready for the dirt on dairy? Dairy is often full of cholesterol and saturated fat and can be tainted with pesticides, hormones, antibiotics, steroids, and even (gulp) blood and pus from infected cows. Dairy has also been linked to cancer, obesity, allergies, constipation, heart disease, and even osteoporosis. When you think about it, our bodies are just not designed to consume dairy products. We only need milk when we are infants. After all, you don't see any adult cows drinking milk. They get all of the calcium they need from vegetable sources, such as grasses and grains.

Calcium is great for your bones, but there is a reason that the countries with the highest consumption of dairy products also have the highest occurrence of osteoporosis. Dairy is loaded with acidic protein, which actually pulls calcium out of your bones in order to regulate the body's pH balance. Your best sources for calcium are foods such as soy, broccoli, figs, chickpeas, kale, almonds, and calcium-enriched juices.

> **TOTAL MOM TIP**
> **Call in**
> **a Sub**

There are some awesome dairy replacements on the market. Veggie Shreds and Veggie Slices are great cheese alternatives, Smart Balance is a tasty margarine for spreading or cooking, Silk is a super soy milk, and Soy Delicious is a totally yummy ice cream replacement that comes in a lot of flavors. Pick up some dairy replacements the next time you are at the grocery store, and I'm sure you will find products that you love.

There is one exception to all this: probiotics. Probiotics are good bacteria that offer health benefits beyond basic nutrition, such as improving the condition of your digestive tract, where 70 percent of your immune system is located. Cultured foods containing probiotics, such as kefir and certain types of yogurt, strengthen your body's defenses and are a great addition to your diet.

C is for Chemicals. They come disguised in all different forms, but for the most part, chemicals are used to enhance and alter food. They may give food a different texture, flavor, or color, or increase its shelf life, and what they do to your health isn't a huge concern for the manufacturer. Become a label reader. If you don't recognize the ingredient, then your digestive system probably won't recognize it either. Start cutting out artificial flavors, colors, and preservatives, and your body will thank you.

Choosing food labeled *organic* is a great way to be sure that you are not inundating your body with harmful chemicals, and more and more food manufacturers are catching on to the needs of health-conscious consumers. Look for organic food in the natural food section of your favorite supermarket or consider shopping at your local health food store.

TOTAL MOM TIP
Chemical Free

If you purchase processed foods, look for natural additives and colorings, such as beets (to give it color) or evaporated cane juice (to make it sweet). If you want a calorie-free sweetener, try using stevia, a natural herbal sweetener.

Here is a short list of some of the more dangerous chemicals present in the average diet. Start the cleansing process by eliminating some or all of them from your diet.

- Acesulfame-k — known commercially as Sweet One or Sunett
- Artificial colors
- Aspartame — known commercially as Equal and Nutrasweet
- Butylated hydroxyanisole (BHA) and butylated hydroxytoluene (BHT)
- Monosodium glutamate (MSG)

- Nitrites and nitrates
- Olestra
- Potassium bromate
- Sulfites

R is for Refined Carbohydrates. Carbohydrates are not the problem; the refinement of carbohydrates is. Our bodies need food in its whole form, not stripped and bleached. The food industry learned early that if you take away the bran, germ, and germ oil from grain and leave all of the nutrient-deficient "fluff," flour and bread look a lot prettier and last a lot longer. Unfortunately, there is always a price to pay. Trying to digest refined food stresses our system and can result in constipation, upset stomach, intestinal blockage and cramping, headaches, behavioral problems, and a weakened immune system. Do your body and your mind a favor and get rid of culprits like white flour, white rice, white sugar, corn syrup, and anything else that looks like a far cry from its natural form.

TOTAL MOM TIP
Whole or Nothin'

Don't be fooled by a label reading "wheat flour." The first ingredient on the label should begin with the word *whole*.

A is for Animal Protein. Stay with me here! I know this is a biggie, but it makes a huge difference to your health. Our entire family eats a strict vegetarian diet, and it feels great! Meat is an extremely dense food that can stress your digestive system, and the majority of meat on the market today is riddled with antibiotics, hormones, pesticides, and other toxic substances. A meat-based diet has been linked to everything from heart disease to cancer. If you are a die-hard meat lover, then just try to make some changes you can live with. To begin with, shop for lean cuts of meat or chicken and fish. Choose the highest grade you can afford and try to stick with organic meat so that you can avoid all the harmful chemicals. Instead of viewing meat as the main course, serve it as a side and supplement it with lots of vegetables. And if you are accustomed to eating meat at every meal, venture into new territory. Pick up some vegetarian cookbooks and try some new recipes.

TOTAL MOM TIP
Veggie Mommy

There are some fantastic meat replacements on the market today. Morningstar Farms and Boca are both great sources for items such as hot dogs, sausage, burgers, meat "crumbles," and even corn dogs. Try some and see what you think.

P is for Processed Foods. "Quick and easy" has become the motto of the typical American diet, but we are paying for it with our health. Processed foods are far removed from their origins. In order to get that beautiful, perfect strawberry to become a strawberry-flavored three-foot-long strip of dried "fruit" paste, it has to be cooked, colored, preserved, emulsified, pumped through a machine, and packaged for your convenience. By the time you eat it, there are no health benefits left.

Whole food is far superior to processed food. Even if processed food is not loaded with chemicals, it is not an ideal choice for your health. There will always be those times when we grab a quick-and-easy snack food, but try to reach for something that is as minimally processed as possible (e.g., natural applesauce rather than colored and sweetened applesauce, dried fruit instead of fruit gummies, corn chips over fried cheese twists). And when you have a choice, go for whole food—food that is still in the form that nature made.

Week Two, Day Five: Daily Exercises

1. In your journal, plan out some of your family's favorite meals for this week but give them a makeover. Make at least two of those meals vegetarian and try to replace unhealthy ingredients, like cheese or white flour, with some healthier alternatives. For an easy way to plan a month's worth of meals, download the Total Mom Monthly Planner from the Web site (TotalMom.com), write out the meals list for the month, slip it into a clear plastic sheet protector, and hang it from three self-adhesive hooks attached to the side of the refrigerator.

2. Practice Actions Skill #1: Piggyback Your Tasks and Actions Skill #6: Reward Yourself. Write down all the errands you need to do this week and choose one day to consolidate them all into one trip. This should include a trip to the grocery store for some healthy ingredients to prepare some family meals. When you go to the grocery store, pick up a healthy treat for yourself (I love soy ice cream!) and find a personal hiding spot in the freezer or cabinet to store it. Now, go ahead and indulge after you finish some chores around the house.

Weekend Workout

Home: Put together a playlist of some of your favorite high-energy songs and begin de-cluttering Zone 1. If you need some ideas, TotalMom.com has a lot of fun playlists to choose from. Remember, the zone has to be something reasonable. Don't try to take on the world in a weekend. This is a good opportunity to practice Action Skill #2: Take Baby Steps. Break down the big project into little, daily steps that are more manageable. Perhaps if Zone 1 is the kitchen, you could de-clutter the bottom cabinets one day, the top cabinets the next day, and so on, until the task is completed.

Health: This is the weekend you begin weeding the seven toxic foods out of your diet. On Saturday your focus area is bad fats. Get some healthy cold-pressed olive oil and replace your shortening or butter with margarine that has no trans fat. Check the labels of your favorite snack foods for bad fat content. And avoid anything deep-fried, especially at fast-food restaurants. Your focus area on Sunday is addictive substances. Try cutting back on the amount of sugar, salt, caffeine, and other addictive substances that are polluting your diet, but remember to take it slow and easy. Just cut back a little bit every day.

Family: Plan a weekend, very soon, for you and your husband to sneak away and reconnect. If a weekend is not an option right now, then at least schedule a night all to yourselves. Hire a babysitter or let the kids spend the night at Grandma's. Here is a book that will give you some creative ideas on ways to get the sparks ignited: *The Great Sex Weekend: A 48-Hour Guide to Rekindling Sparks for Bold, Busy, or Bored Lovers* by Pepper Schwartz and Janet Lever.

Life: Purchase a new, comfortable pair of shoes that looks sharp (way better than those old, dirty sneakers with worn-out arches). A good choice would be yoga shoes or some trendy sneakers. Make it a point this week to get up, get fully dressed and de-frumped, put on your new butt-kicking shoes, and get to work creating the life that you envision.

Congratulations!

You have built a strong and healthy foundation for a whole new you. Your basic needs—food, sleep, sex, shelter, and clothing—are now being met in the best way possible. With your tank fueled up, you are ready to move on to Week Three.

SECURE MOM

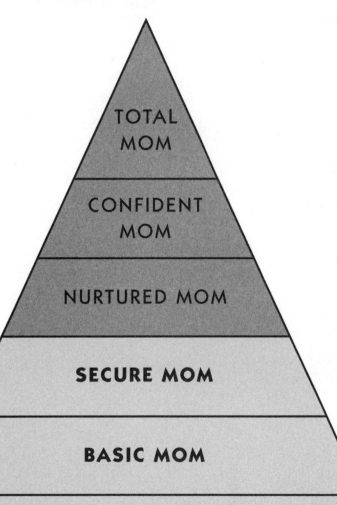

TOTAL
MOM

CONFIDENT
MOM

NURTURED MOM

SECURE MOM

BASIC MOM

STARTER MOM

Who's Afraid?

The Secure Mom has met her basic needs today, and she is meeting her needs for tomorrow as well. But tomorrow holds the unknown, and that can be frightening and chaotic at times. Fear keeps you enslaved, and chaos robs you of peace. The best way to face tomorrow is to establish security today. And it all begins right now.

Fear can keep you from experiencing so much of life, and no one knows fear like a mother. My life changed dramatically when I saw those two pink stripes on the pregnancy test. It was as if the lens through which I viewed the world was suddenly replaced with another. I quickly became a blurry spot in the distance, and all that mattered was this tiny life growing within me. I had a new focal point in life, a bright star around which everything in my own private universe would revolve. It was an instant and irreversible shift. Motherhood has a way of doing that—changing a woman's entire outlook on life and self. It was, and still is, exhilarating and terrifying at the same time.

Motherhood means going from a linear existence to a life of extremes—extreme certainty and extreme confusion, extreme bliss and extreme fear. And nothing can immobilize us faster than fear. There's a lot to be afraid of when it comes to parenting. When it's just you, you can usually hush those demons that whisper their empty threats. But when you become a mother, everything around you grows horns and a forked tongue. Fear backs you into a corner, and then you are in a position that every mother knows intimately—stuck. And if you are ever going to be able to stride confidently into tomorrow, then you need to pull your feet out of the fear that holds you back. Getting unstuck requires two things—knowledge and action.

Thinking Through Your Fears

The thing about maternal fears is that our perception isn't always based in reality. We are terrified that someone will kidnap our children, but we often don't give a moment's thought to our children getting skin cancer. The chance of your child ever being reported missing (not necessarily kidnapped, but simply reported missing for any number of reasons) by you or someone else, is less than one in a hundred. However, one out of every four people will be diagnosed with skin cancer, most likely caused by sun exposure—and 80 percent of all sun exposure occurs before the age of eighteen. The risk of getting skin cancer far outweighs the risk of getting kidnapped, but our minds don't always accept reality. Instead, our fears feed on the unknown. That's why the first step you should take to face your fears is to understand them.

Name your fears. Don't think that by voicing a fear you will coax it into occurring. Actually, it's quite the opposite. The more you deny your fears, the more negative energy you put toward that perceived threat. Your thoughts affect your actions, and you can begin behaving in a way that makes that threat a reality. You may be terrified of traffic and scared to death of letting your child cross a street by himself. Through your words and your actions, you instill this fear in your child. When it comes time to cross a street, instead of thinking logically and acting intelligently, he panics and runs.

After you name your fears, start doing some research. When you begin educating yourself, you will probably find that the worries you deal with are not founded in reality but in your imagination. By feeding

"Nothing in life is to be feared. It is only to be understood."
— MARIE CURIE

your mind real facts, you will lessen the impact of this fear on your life as well as establish a positive way to deal with your fears effectively.

Acting on Your Fears

One way to send your fears running is to begin taking action. As you approach your fears, the dark shadow that they cast over your life gets smaller and smaller until you are left with something real and tangible, something you can learn from and leverage to become a better mom. For example, if you are scared of your child being the victim of drunk driving, then join MADD and help the organization. Educate your children about the dangers and potential risks of drunk driving. Attend an event that supports the cause. Become a political advocate for instituting harsher penalties for DUIs. By taking action, your fear is lessened and your risk decreased.

**TOTAL MOM TIP
Don't Join
the Anxiety
Society**

There are moms everywhere who jump from fear to fear, dragging plenty of other women along with them. They are members of the "Anxiety Society." One way to make your fear grow to astronomical proportions is to feed it with fret, and the Anxiety Society does just that. These moms sit around and fret—talking "sex offenders" one minute and "bird flu" the next. It's ideal to have a support network of other moms, but only if it serves to enrich who you are and how you perform as a mother. We need to share our fears and discuss dangers, but once a topic moves from informative to distressing, it's time to move on and carry the conversation into a brighter light.

Don't remain a victim of fears and worries that you have fabricated. Don't let your emotions control you. Control your emotions. Instead of shutting your fears behind a door and trying your best to keep it locked, throw the door open. Let them spill out and get in the very middle of them. Touch them, feel them, hold them, and learn all you can about them. As a mom you will never be without worries, so embrace your fears. Fear is good for us when it propels us into positive and productive action.

Common Mommy Monsters

There are some common fears and worries that dance through every mom's nightmares. We don't want to discuss them. We don't even want to acknowledge them. We feel that these monsters are somehow contagious, that if we familiarize ourselves with these monsters or their victims, then we may be next. It doesn't work that way. Knowledge is power, and action is the execution of that power. Empower yourself by meeting your monsters.

Fear of Failure

So many moms have these amazing talents and abilities that they could be sharing with the world. They have stories to tell, products to invent, movements to lead, businesses to run. The problem occurs when we let that fear of failure prevent us from trying our wings at something. We allow this fear to hold us back as individuals and also as mothers. We are so frightened that we are going to screw up our children. Well, I'm pretty sure we all will at one time or another. If we are not too strict, then we are too lenient—that's the whole push-pull dance that makes up about 95 percent of parenting.

Knowledge and Action: The fear of failure can be healthy because it prevents us from leaping before we look and messing up—big time! But if we spend all our time looking, we are going to miss out on life. Go ahead and accept the possibility of failure and free yourself up to fly. If you are scared to jump full force into a project, then play around a little with it on the side. If you are afraid of starting that greeting card business, then why not just make a few samples and see if they sell at the next craft show? And keep in mind that we all fail at some time or another, especially when it comes to the clearly undefined career of motherhood. Don't let that fear prevent you from parenting. Keep communicating with your children, keep trying your best, keep making mistakes and learning from them.

Fear of the Unknown

It strikes us daily. What if a huge storm hits my town? What if my husband loses his job? What if my child does poorly in school? These fears plague us for the same reason we look in the mirror and anxiously trace those wrinkles that are beginning to appear. It's not a storm, job loss, poor performance in school, or old age that is scaring us. It's that we don't know what to expect on the other side.

Knowledge and Action: This fear can be healthy when it drives us to learn and grow. Get the down and dirty details on anything that scares you. Are you scared of a storm? Then do some research and find out how to prepare for a weather emergency. Are you scared of unemployment? Talk to some people who have been there or build up a business on the side as a safety net. Are you scared of getting old? Hang with the Red Hat Society, those exciting women who show that fun starts at fifty.

What we can't learn, we must embrace. Your fears of the unknown are probably much larger than the reality they represent. I was scared to death of my husband losing his job, until he did. I didn't think we could make it through a month of unemployment. And then we lasted through a year. It was extremely difficult, but we made it. And today I am grateful for the experience because it taught me so much — about careers, survival, life, and, most important, faith. Life experiences have taught me to loosen my grip and embrace the future with anticipation instead of fear. When you get down to the most basic truth, none of us has any idea what the next moment of life holds. We must learn how to be comfortable with not knowing, and that secret lies in faith. If you believe there is a loving force guiding your life and your family, you can usually sit in the same room with the future without squirming. It's embracing the unknown, not controlling it, that should be your primary focus.

TOTAL MOM TIP
Visualize This!

If you have a fear that keeps haunting you, try practicing some visualization techniques to lessen the hold it has over you. Visualize that fear clearly in your head or visualize someone or something that represents that fear. Imagine it life-size, facing you. Now clearly imagine it getting smaller and smaller, the color draining from it. Finally, it is colorless and so small you can cup it in your hands. What does it look like? How does it sound? Now take a deep breath, blow it away, and watch it evaporate into nothing.

Fear of Harm

Moms are genetically engineered to put their children before themselves. We go to all lengths to keep our family members safe from harm, and with good reason. It's our job, but it can get awfully scary at times. This is the fear that fuels all those neurotic scenarios that play out in our heads. I have spent many hours lying awake at night wondering how I would get the kids evacuated if a huge meteor ever struck the earth, or how I would feed the family in the case of a worldwide famine, or how I would get the kids to safety if my car should ever go careering off a bridge into the water below. Irrational? Of course it is. But that doesn't make these threats feel any less real.

Knowledge and Action: This is probably the healthiest fear because it keeps us on top of our game. But it should propel us to be careful, not fearful. Drain the fear out of potential threats by taking measures to reduce your risk. For example, if you're scared of a fire, then make sure you have an escape route planned. If you're worried about illness, then practice a healthy diet and lifestyle. Understand the difference between controlling your fear and allowing it to control you. For example, controlling your fear is getting a safe car seat and driving without distractions, such as talking on a cell phone. Being controlled by fear is staying at home because you are scared to put your baby in the car and go to the grocery store. When you find that fear is controlling you, take action to stop the negative spiral. Dip your feet in your fear and get wet. If you're scared to take your baby out to the grocery store, then begin by visiting a friend who lives close by. If your fear is completely irrational, then try practicing the Six Steps to a Power Attitude from Week One, Day Five. The trick to handling bizarre fears is to take action to disrupt the train of thought, not necessarily to lessen the threat. Even a little action, such as doing a yoga stretch or stepping outside for some fresh air, is usually enough to disrupt the negative thoughts and replace them with positive ones.

Week Three, Day One: Daily Exercises

1. In your journal, write down the fears that you are currently struggling with, allowing plenty of space between them to jot down notes. Next to each one, write down a plan of attack for facing that fear. How can you apply action in order to reduce your anxiety? After you have listed some steps you need to take, make sure you take them. For example, if you are afraid of your marriage deteriorating, then perhaps you can schedule a date night once a week or spend time together in the evenings without television or other distractions. Schedule it, write it down in your day planner, and follow through.

2. Look over your fears and consider how much time and energy they have robbed from you because of unnecessary worrying and

unproductive anxiety. Take a few minutes and pray that these fears be lifted and carried by a power that is greater than you. Visualize this weight being lifted off your shoulders and feel your wings unfold.

3. This is the day to focus on eliminating or reducing the amount of dairy that you consume. Try out some nondairy replacements like soy milk and soy cheese.

Money Suckers

No matter what you may have heard, ignorance is NOT bliss. Little leaks spring up in our lives and drain out some of our most precious resources. And when we are unaware of them, they can do some serious damage. There is absolutely nothing blissful about that. To get the most out of life, you need to manage all of your resources effectively and efficiently.

Assets and Liabilities

When it came to anything financial, I used to run away faster than you could say "mutual fund." My theory was that I did not need to learn about money. That was left up to men who wore bow ties and women in boxy navy blue suits. However, after surviving and thriving through bankruptcy and plunging myself into business ownership, I learned that what you don't know can kill you, and what doesn't kill you makes you stronger (and much smarter).

The whole language of assets and liabilities always sounded so formal to me. If you are talking shoe fashion or diaper absorbency, then I'm in my comfort zone. But assets and liabilities? No way. I finally wised up and realized that all of my resources, whether money, time, or energy, can be broken down into two things: assets and liabilities. Assets add. Liabilities subtract. And in order to reach a personal level of success with your life, home, health, and family, it's important to focus on accumulating assets and eliminating liabilities. It's the math of life.

Adding It Up

Assets are those financial investments that add to your life. One day I was playing a money management game with the kids. One of them would think of something to buy, and the rest of them would try to think of a way to turn it into an asset that makes you money. One of the older girls said, "Blue jeans," and after some creative brainstorming, they decided you could embellish them with sequins or paint designs on them and then sell them for more money. Another said, "Party decorations"—we had just had a birthday party, so the decorations were still up—and the rest of them suggested that you could start a party-planning business and reuse the decorations to plan parties for money. This continued until one of the boys said, "Xbox," and then said he could charge his friends to play games on it (I quickly threw in a lesson on friendship to supplement the curriculum).

But the math is obvious. Your money is either coming in to your life or leaving your life. The trick is to get more coming in than going out, and to do this you need to either make more money or spend less money. Making money is sometimes the biggest challenge for moms. For years I struggled with this, constantly feeling that I wasn't contributing enough to the family. I then realized that although I was not making money, I was indeed saving it. Instead of bringing in a check, I was, in essence, making tax-free income by saving money on day care, cleaning expenses, and many other things. If you are a stay-at-home mom, then you are doing the most valuable, most important job of all. No career out there holds a candle to what you are investing your life energy into. No paycheck could ever encompass the remarkable work that you are doing.

However, if you feel the burden to contribute financially, or you just want to further your career or personal development, then find that one thing that you absolutely love to do and figure out a way to turn it into cash. I love to write, so I began by simply publishing a newsletter for moms and charging subscriptions. That was eons ago, and now there are more work-from-home opportunities than ever before. We live in a great age for women who want to devote their lives to motherhood while still investing in their careers. If you love to design clothes, then start your own online store and sell your creations over the Internet. If you have a consulting service, then do it over the phone or on the computer. If you would rather not put the time or energy into a start-up company, then there are many reputable direct marketing opportunities for you. Just find your passion and follow it.

> **TOTAL MOM TIP**
> **Stick to**
> **the List**
>
> When you go shopping, don't just wander aimlessly with an empty cart. Make a list and stick to it. Even if you're not grocery shopping, it's important to get what you came for. If you see something is on sale or you notice a cool buy, keep in mind that you were just fine before. You didn't need it then, and you don't need it now. This is especially important in those huge megastores, where you can easily spend $200 and not remember what you came for in the first place.

The Lie of Liabilities

Liabilities pull money out of your pocket. Many of our purchases are just lies that we buy into. We believe they will enrich our lives or fix a problem, but they really just rob us of space, security, and peace of mind. That's the lie, and many of us go through our lives believing it.

So many purchases out there are money suckers. They don't just take your money, they clutter up your life and your mind. Often when we think that we don't have enough money, the real problem is that we don't have enough self-control. Get your vision in focus. If you want more for your future, then you need to make smart purchases today. I have seen huge satellite dishes resting outside of dilapidated homes. Something is off balance there; the owner sees the gratification of watching television today and not of having a beautiful home tomorrow.

Chances are, you are the one holding the purse strings. Research has shown that moms are responsible for more than 85 percent of a family's purchases. Therefore, most of the responsibility lies in your hands. But it doesn't stop there. When you are the one managing the money, you are also the one setting a pattern of behavior that your kids are scrutinizing, whether you realize it or not. Your children will understand what is important to you by the way you spend your money. They will see that you have big plans for yourself and your family when you pass on the purchase in order to put more into the college fund. They will see you comparing prices and making smart choices. They will see you go for quality over quantity. And, most important, they will see you making choices today that will get you where you want to be tomorrow.

When you see those items that you've just gotta have, remember that if you buy them, the money is pulled from something else. It could come out of that larger home you want, the business you've been itching to start, or something else that has better long-term value. Don't cheapen your hopes and dreams by selling them off for transient little goodies that thrill you one moment and clutter up your life the next. Go for the big prize.

Little Leaks

There are a lot of money suckers out there that sneak in undetected. Little things like that daily cappuccino, late fees, fast food, or other quick and thoughtless little purchases can really add up. Suddenly, you look at your balance and wonder, where did it all go? David Bach, an author and speaker on finance, refers to this in his books as "the Latte Factor."

He suggests that the difference between accumulating wealth and living paycheck to paycheck lies in our small daily purchases, such as the latte on the way to work. If we become aware of these purchases and redirect our spending, we could change our financial future completely.

A latte and a muffin cost about $5—not that much money. But when you consider that just $5 a day invested at a rate of 10 percent annual return would yield $948,611 in forty years, you can see how important the little expenditures are. Little leaks can sink big ships. Don't let those purchases rob you of peace of mind. Think about every purchase—the little ones as much as the big ones. The money that you have is the result of effort, either yours or someone else's. Is it worth selling that effort for that insignificant little purchase? When you spend your money, make it count.

I overhear a lot of people complaining about being "broke." This term suggests much more than just financial poverty. It suggests mental and emotional poverty as well. Remember to keep using your tool of communication. Even if you feel financially challenged, use words that have the ability to transform your reality and thus encourage you to transform your life. *Broke* should be crossed out of your vocabulary. Replace it with words that enable you to do something about your situation—*challenged, growing, learning, saving.*

Three Simple Questions

I know as well as the next mom how hard it is to pass up a good deal. However, sometimes a good deal now can be a big problem later, when you are low on funds and the bills are flying in. Before you make a purchase, ask yourself these three simple questions:

1. **Do I need this?** Many times our needs get clouded over by our wants. Your needs are what you worked on last week, those items that are

necessary for a healthy life — healthy food, an enriching home, and other items that you can't thrive without (and no, even if they are on sale, those Jimmy Choos are not considered a need).

2. **Can I make it or use something I already have?** Most purchases can be passed up because we have what we need already. Cut off your old sweatpants instead of buying athletic shorts. Sew a comforter instead of buying one. Make a pizza instead of ordering takeout. Paint an old picture frame instead of purchasing a new one. A little creativity can save you lots of cash.

3. **Will this purchase help me reach my vision?** This is why it is so important to develop a clear vision of who you are becoming. It will guide you through many of your purchases. For example, if you see yourself living in a big house, then you will be more likely to put that toy back on the shelf in order to get to a financial standing where you can purchase the house. If you have plenty of money for purchases, this question can still guide you on your spending patterns. If you have a clear vision of family unity, then you will be more likely to spend your money on items that foster togetherness, such as board games or a family vacation. If you have a clear vision of increasing your wealth, you will look for investment purchases, such as real estate or business ventures. If you have a clear vision of dressing stylishly, then yes, you can grab those Jimmy Choos.

The Trappings of Today

One of my close friends often complains about her financial situation and how she never has any money. But the truth is she would have plenty of money if she only knew how to hold on to it. She has a problem that many of us suffer from — being trapped. These trappings take all different forms. It could be a new pair of jeans or an extra throw rug, maybe some toys for the kids or a better television. The problem occurs when these traps prevent you from living the life that you deserve. I visited my friend shortly after Christmas and was astonished by the sheer mass of gifts that she and her husband had bought for their kids. They all had their own game system (to go with their own television), as well as lots of new clothes and toys. Their tiny living room was literally packed so full of presents that you couldn't even see the floor. And meanwhile, she was suffering from stress headaches because they couldn't pay their bills.

Don't let the trappings of today prevent you from living your vision for the future. Money may seem to buy happiness, but that happiness is fleeting. The toy that thrills your child one day bores him the next. Real joy lies in living a life that is in line with your dreams and goals. Straining yourself financially robs you of peace and ensnares you in a sticky web of fear and anxiety. You deserve to be free of the trappings. Nothing you can buy feels as good as freedom from financial worries.

TOTAL MOM TIP
Saving Here,
Saving There

Every time you save or spend money, you affect much more than just your personal finances. It's all connected. When you take measures to save money, you often affect your health and the environment for the better, while spending money can have the opposite effect. For example, buying a candy bar takes money away from you. It damages your health with poor nutrition. It supports large factories that pollute the environment and produces waste that will be added to a landfill. You can see this relationship all over your finances. The less we buy, the smaller impact we make on this earth and the better our health is by not living with excess. Of course, you don't need to live out of a shopping cart, but it's something to think about.

Money does matter, a great deal. The way you manage your money is a reflection of your life principles. Start making choices today that will help you reach your financial dreams tomorrow.

Week Three, Day Two: Daily Exercises

1. In your journal, think through your average day and write down the money suckers in your life. Do you indulge in a daily latte? Can you replace it with some coffee that you doctor up at home? Can you replace dinner out for an inexpensive (and probably healthier) homemade meal? Instead of spending an evening at the theater, could you go for a matinee or rent a video instead? Next to every money sucker, write down a less expensive replacement that you can begin using. An easy way to get started is to replace all of your store-bought cereal with some homemade (and much healthier) granola. You can find a great recipe at TotalMom.com.

2. Managing your finances is a lifelong process. Ignorance is not bliss, so begin educating yourself to ensure the most productive and prosperous future possible. Check out some books on finance that will help you grow in this area. Here are some suggestions:

Rich Dad, Poor Dad. What the Rich Teach Their Kids About Money — That the Poor and Middle Class Do Not! by Robert T. Kiyosaki, with Sharon L. Lechter

The 9 Steps to Financial Freedom: Practical and Spiritual Steps So You Can Stop Worrying by Suze Orman

Smart Women Finish Rich: 9 Steps to Achieving Financial Security and Funding Your Dreams by David Bach

3. This is the day that you can begin eliminating all those chemicals from your diet. Look through your cabinets and your refrigerator and toss out some of those artificial colors, flavors, and preservatives (if not all of them). It's time to feel like a natural woman! Remember to get some tasty organic replacements so that the kids won't be tempted to stage a mutiny.

Mommy 911

Children have an uncanny knack for being little angels one moment and little demons the next. It's enough to make any decent, God-fearing, law-abiding mother go ballistic. But take a deep breath and put down your weapons. Freeing yourself from chaos and insecurity means knowing that you are doing right by your children, today and tomorrow. You should be enjoying this time with your kids, not struggling over behavior issues. If you feel like your home frequently morphs into a battlefield, then try heeding some dos and don'ts from someone who has been there and done that.

DO Listen

It's easy for a mom to fall into the trap of thinking her way is not only the right way but the only way. This belief eventually leads to closed ears and, worse, a closed heart. It is your job to teach your children. But motherhood comes with the added benefit of learning from them as well. Our children have a great deal to teach us, if we only let them.

One of the most important keys to managing your children's behavior is to listen to them. If we truly take the time and attention necessary to tune in to our children's needs, we can better understand how to handle misbehavior when it occurs. Listen to them with an open mind and

115

an open heart. This means keeping quiet when that voice of judgment wants to speak up. Because we are adults, we have a tendency to impose our own plans and standards on our children. Approach them with the intention of learning. Ask them about their feelings, their opinions, and the rationale behind their behavior. Communication is a two-way street, so don't do all the talking. If you do, you're going to miss out on one of the most rewarding aspects of the mother-child relationship.

Keep in mind that communication isn't just verbal. I have one daughter who hardly takes time to catch her breath between sentences, while another is quiet and introspective. Learn to read your children and speak their language. If one is more verbal, then take the time to listen and talk. If another is less verbal, then her language may be to play games or work on projects with you. Know your child inside and out and keep those lines of communication open. The best way to deal with disobedience is to understand where it stems from. Our children will tell us if we take the time to listen.

DON'T Threaten

Threats are made in anger, and they do nothing except frustrate parents and confuse children. When you threaten, you limit yourself to two choices: Follow through with the threat, or look like an idiot. If you follow through, you have taught them that anger is a viable option, which it should never be. If you end up looking like an idiot, then you have taught them that you don't always mean what you say and that disobedience is acceptable. Don't resort to threats. You are smarter than that. Establish a cause and effect before the frustrating situation ever has a chance to present itself. Don't let anger get the best of you by reacting to a situation instead of intelligently responding to it. Here are some common "threat traps" to avoid,

- ◉ **1-2-3:** This is the behavior countdown that I see so many moms do. A child is misbehaving, so the mom tells the child to stop.

The child doesn't stop, so the mom begins counting. When she gets to the number three, one of two things occurs. The child's misbehavior stops, and she learns that misbehavior is acceptable to a certain, undefined level. Or the misbehavior doesn't stop and the mom usually repeats herself, teaching nothing constructive in the process. Instead of counting, tell your child what you expect of him and apply consequences if necessary. If your child is very young, he might need help to follow through. For example, if he needs to put a toy down, explain why (we have to leave, someone else wants to play with it, etc.). If he refuses, take it away. No cajoling, no threatening, no drama.

◎ **I'm leaving you:** This threat is just cruel. When your child doesn't want to leave a place, it simply means he is intrigued by something. Try to be understanding. Explain why you must leave, give him some incentive to leave, or even pick him up and carry him out; but don't ever resort to telling him that you are going to leave him. First, it is dishonest. Even though you may feel like doing it sometimes, you would never leave your child. Second, this threat uses fear to shape behavior, and it's fear of the worst kind—a fear of abandonment. Your job as a mother is to impart security and trust—never fear. Make transition easier on children by giving them a warning signal. Always give them "one more" of something, even before they get a chance to argue. At the playground, let them pick two more activities before you leave. At the pool, let them jump off the diving board three more times. At Chuck E. Cheese's, give them ten more minutes. By preparing them, you are paving the way for a smooth exit. It's like the yellow light before the inevitable red.

DO Allow Consequences

You are doing an injustice to your child if you spare her the natural consequences of her behavior. If she can't keep her toys picked up, then maybe she doesn't deserve the privilege of playing with them. If she can't get ready in time for the bus, then maybe she needs to miss it and walk into class late. It may seem cruel at times, but the more we coddle our children, the more we strip them of valuable lessons they can learn only through natural consequences.

TOTAL MOM TIP
A Point on Pointing

When you point one finger, you've got more fingers pointing back at you! Pointing is a nonverbal way to communicate blame and fault, as well as one more way of attempting to establish a pecking order between you and the kids. If you must use your hands to communicate, then use them to gently turn your child's face to yours so that you can establish eye contact when you are speaking, which is very important when giving instruction.

"In spite of the seven thousand books of expert advice, the right way to discipline a child is still a mystery to most.... Only your grandmother and Ghengis Khan know how to do it."

—BILL COSBY

We never grow out of this lesson. I have toddlers ("Oops! You threw your crayons. I guess you can't color anymore") as well as teenagers ("Oops! You didn't do laundry. I guess you'll have to wear your dirty jeans") who are still learning it. Teaching children responsibility is extremely important. When you cajole, plead, and remind over and over, you are teaching them that they don't have to be responsible for their behavior. Help them develop an internal navigation system to make their way through life by allowing natural consequences as much as possible.

DON'T Label

When working on behavior issues, keep in mind that you want to reprimand the negative behavior, not the child. Call attention to what he did that was wrong, not to him as a person. For example, if your child hits another, then make sure to say that hitting is bad, not that he is bad.

Steer clear of all-encompassing statements that begin with "you are," unless they are intended to build the child up instead of tear him down.

Even if it is a character trait that you need to address, make sure that you do not ridicule the child. For example, with hitting, instead of saying, "You are so mean. What is wrong with you?" a better choice would be, "You seem to be acting very mean today. What is bothering you?" By labeling the behavior and not the child, you are separating that behavior from your child's nature.

Always assume the best in your child. If you radiate the belief that your child is genuinely good and loving, then the misbehaviors become exceptions. Go ahead and label those negative behaviors. When you address them and talk about them with your child, you can help him work them out. This works especially well when you preface your instruction with the character traits that you want to see. For example, "You really love your brother, and you are a kind person. So why are you choosing to hit him?" Give your child the freedom to develop into a remarkable person by avoiding labels that define him in negative ways.

TOTAL MOM TIP
Teachable Moments

Avoid the "heat of the moment" attempts to change your child's behavior. The best time to deal with the negative behavior is when it's not occurring. Pick a time when everything is running smoothly to address the behavior that needs to be modified. This works especially well with older children. Often, when a child is misbehaving, the logical part of her brain is taking a leave of absence. Any words you say to her while she's in that state may as well be spoken in Latin (provided your kids don't speak Latin). Get control of the behavior but don't go into a big lecture about it. The best time to approach the topic is when your child is calm and compliant. You want to engage your child in a discussion, not preach a sermon. This is one example where timing is everything.

DO Be an Adult

Often, the best piece of advice for moms is to *grow up!* Just because children can act like brats doesn't mean you should. Even when they are driving you crazy, remember that you are the adult in the relationship. And when the going gets tough, you've got to step up to the plate and act your age. I've seen moms get into screaming matches with their children, mock their behaviors, whine, cry, and stomp their feet in frustration. It's like watching one child trying to raise another. Where is the grown-up?

As a mom, you have an awesome responsibility, not one to be taken lightly. No matter how frustrated, angry, or overwhelmed you get, you do not have the luxury of acting like a child. You are the adult, and you must remain the adult. You are the person the little ones are looking to for confidence, trust, comfort, and guidance. When you do feel the control slipping, try to remove yourself from the situation before it gets any worse. Remember to pause for a moment and respond intelligently to

TOTAL MOM TIP
Water
Babies

I have a great tip passed down to me from my mother. Whenever a child was getting on her nerves, she would just stick *her* in the bath. I say *her* because I am the youngest of five children, all girls except for one, my brother, Charles, who seemed incapable of disobedience. We got in trouble a lot, but Mom never reacted. Instead, she responded with a bath full of warm water. We had to sit in the bath until Mom eventually regained control and could deal lovingly with the situation, which was usually when the water reached subarctic temperatures. Needless to say, we were the wrinkliest kids on the block. But Mom was right. It works. My own kids have been waterlogged on several occasions. Something about a warm bubble bath just soothes the spirit. So maybe after the kids have calmed down, you can enjoy one yourself!

the situation instead of just reacting to it. You are the one in control, and you have to handle that responsibility intelligently. Don't react to your child with the same negative attitude that she may have demonstrated. You are above that. If she is frustrated, you must remain calm. If she is angry, you must remain amicable. It may try your patience, but it is imperative that you remain in control.

DON'T Push Their Limits

Sometimes the best thing you can do as a mom is ease up a little. Continually challenge your children to grow, but don't overwhelm them with responsibility. Like everyone, they have their limits, so try not to push them too hard. If your daughter has taken piano for three years and doesn't want to pursue it any longer, then let her test her wings on something else. If your son hates spending the night away from home, then give him an easy out by offering to pick him up late at night. If your toddler gets tired in the afternoon, then don't choose that time to take him shopping.

The fact is, in some situations a mom's expectations have to play second fiddle. You may want your daughter to be an accomplished musician. You may want your son to go to Scout camp like everyone else. You may want to go shopping in the afternoon. But a child has limits, and they need to be acknowledged and respected. Sometimes you just need to let it go. Communicate, assist, and, above all, try to understand. The world takes on a completely different perspective when you look at it through your child's eyes.

Week Three, Day Three: Daily Exercises

1. In your journal, write down some areas of child behavior management that need improvement. Are you too quick to react? Do you listen enough? Do you allow for natural consequences? After you write down some problem areas, think of things you can do that are more effective. Can you pause and count to ten before you respond? Can you set aside some time each day to spend in conversation with your child? Can you step back from a certain situation in which your child needs to develop more responsibility and allow for natural consequences? Write these down, visualize yourself responding to your child effectively, and establish a game plan so that you can be prepared for misbehavior when it rears its ugly head.

2. With all the research on behavior modification, one fact still holds true: Positive reinforcement is still the most effective way to shape behavior. Set up a system in your home to reward your child for good behavior and personal responsibility. If you go to TotalMom.com, you can download a behavior chart to serve as an end-of-the-day checklist for your child. You can also customize your own chart by listing daily goals for your child in the area of behavior and personal responsibility (e.g., Brushes Teeth, Makes Up Bed, Obeys Mommy and Daddy, Has a Good Attitude, etc.). Whatever goals you choose for your child, make sure that you have no more than ten, or else it will get too confusing. Let each goal equal one point, and when they get all of their points, give them a reward, such as a sticker.

3. This is the day to focus on cutting back on your refined carbs. Go through your cereals, breads, and pastas and look for the word *whole* as the first ingredient on the label, such as *whole* oat flour or *whole* wheat flour. If it's not there, then the product is refined and lacks the necessary fiber that your body needs. Look for healthy replacements at the grocery store.

Get Your Rear in Gear

You can create a better tomorrow by making the best use of today. Get a head start on shaping your life—and your body—by getting up and getting going. Life-changing moments often go by unnoticed. They happen when you show the discipline to live life to the fullest and make the most out of your mind, body, and spirit. Those little daily steps forward are the moments that really define us and determine our path. They happen when we put back that second cookie, when we turn off the TV and sit on the floor for a pretend tea party, when we wash the dishes before we leave the kitchen, and when we roll out of bed and get our bodies going instead of getting a few more minutes of sleep.

Head Start

Back in grade school, we always wanted to be at the head of the line. We knew if we were getting in a line, there must be something worth getting. Even if we were just going outside for recess or to the cafeteria for some chocolate pudding, we knew instinctively that there was an advantage to being first. And we were right.

When you get up early, you beat the crowds. You are getting ahead of the game and using your time to your advantage. When you roll out of bed and go walking or exercise to a video, you are choosing to achieve a goal and get ahead of those who are letting life pass them by. You are not just living a life, you are fully experiencing it. You are *totally* alive.

It also helps to get a head start when you have little ones in the home. Being a full-time mom often means that entire days go by without a single moment to yourself. You have to make a deliberate effort to carve out some time for you. Getting up before everyone else guarantees that you get your time. Let the others sleep. You have a life to live and a body to get moving. This is the time to charge up your battery so that you can be everything you need to be for yourself and your family. Your AM routine benefits not only you but everyone else in your home.

TOTAL MOM TIP
Spoil Yourself

A little selfish motivation goes a long way when you are beginning the practice of waking up early. Buy something special for yourself that will help you get your day started. For example, if you would like to spend a few minutes painting in the mornings, then buy some quality watercolors and some bristol board to motivate you to get out of bed. To get you psyched for your morning walk, buy yourself some new workout clothes so that you will look good and feel good. A purchase like this is definitely in line with the vision you have for yourself.

Full-Body Advantage

Getting up early can benefit your entire body. It will give your mind some quiet time to think and plan. And it will help your body if you use that time to squeeze in some exercise. Exercise will help you have more energy, get in shape, keep up with your kids and your lifestyle, and strengthen your immune system so that you stay healthy. And as an added benefit, it feels great! At first your body might dig in its heels and resist any change you are trying to make. But eventually exercise will be one of the highlights of your day — I guarantee it.

People today often have a warped idea of exercise, because even in our advanced age of technology, the human race is more sedentary than ever. Instead of a way of living, physical activity has become a separate task crammed into our already crowded schedules. We have become lazy and, in return, are suffering from obesity, fatigue, depression, and a host of diseases. With no time to exercise, we set aside forty-five minutes every few days to take in a brutal exercise class. But we drive to the facility, take the elevator to the correct floor, and then sit down outside and wait for the class to begin. On top of all that, we pay good money to accomplish this. It doesn't make much sense to spend our time and money on something that we could do for free and with much more pleasure throughout our average workday.

Of course, sometimes you have to set aside time for specific exercise, like training for a sporting event or getting rid of that postpartum flab. But for the vast majority of moms, the best exercise program consists of simply living a more active life. Look for opportunities to get up and get moving and grooving. Maybe you and the kids can play a game of tag in the backyard, or perhaps you can go on a nice long walk in the morning. Whatever you choose to do for exercise, make sure that it is something you totally enjoy so that you are more likely to continue it.

Think F.I.T.

To get the maximum benefit out of any exercise program, you need to make sure that it is challenging enough to get you in shape and keep you in shape while still being enjoyable. You also need to make sure that it is not too challenging. If the program is too difficult, you will be more likely to abandon it. Ensure that it meets your needs by thinking F.I.T.

F is for Frequency. You should begin by getting some exercise at least three times a week. As you adjust to this level, increase the frequency of your workout until you are exercising five to seven times a week.

"Welcome every morning with a smile. Look on the new day as another special gift from your Creator, another golden opportunity to complete what you were unable to finish yesterday. Be a self-starter. Let your first hour set the theme of success and positive action that is certain to echo through your entire day. Today will never happen again. Don't waste it with a false start or no start at all. You were not born to fail."
—OG MANDINO

I is for Intensity. Intensity measures the difficulty of your exercise program. Remember, you don't have to sweat bullets or pull a muscle just to be in shape. You want your workout to increase your heart rate while still allowing you to breathe and talk easily. Walking is ideal because you can begin slowly, but pick up the pace or add some arm weights as your ability improves.

T is for Time. How long should you work out? Six minutes or sixty minutes? Ideally, go for twenty minutes of activity, but feel free to adjust this depending on your fitness level, and increase it gradually. Your workout should leave you energized, not exhausted.

As you make exercise a daily habit, remember to adjust your program according to your F.I.T. levels. Work out longer, harder, or more frequently in order to keep yourself continually challenged. And if you find that you get stuck in a rut, then don't hesitate to switch things up a bit and try new activities. Fitness should be a way of life, so make it enjoyable.

Determination, Not Motivation

Motivation only goes so far. It's nice to feel strong and empowered, but I will be the first to admit that there are days when I am just not feeling motivated to put on my walking shoes. Nothing can get me excited about walking two miles on a cold, wet February morning. But these are the times when I have to remind myself that it's not about getting excited or motivated. It's about achieving my goal of being healthy and doing what I set out to do. This is where motivation has little or nothing to do with behavior, and everything comes down to gut determination.

Determination comes into play when every obstacle in the world stands in your way but you are so focused on your goals that you grit your teeth, close your eyes, and do what needs to be done. It means setting your sights on the horizon and putting one foot in front of the other in order to get there. Motivation is feeling compelled to do what you should do. Determination is doing it even when you're not motivated. It has nothing to do with emotion but everything to do with resolve.

Feeling physically and mentally alive every day requires a conscious decision. It means living with a deliberate intent to get as much as you can out of every day. It means living juicy and resolving never, ever to let your body, mind, or spirit stagnate and dry up. Wake up! Feel alive! Live juicy!

Week Three, Day Four: Daily Exercises

1. In your journal, write down at least ten reasons why you should get up before anyone else in the house. Remember, if the "why" is important enough, then the "how" usually takes care of itself. Think about all of the times that you feel rushed to get ready in the morning and frustrated with yourself or your kids. Some of the reasons I get up early are to have peaceful mornings, to be prepared for the day, to exercise and get my energy up, and simply to have some time all to myself. This list will help you keep your determination when your motivation has run for the hills.

2. We all need a little help now and then to keep up a regular exercise program. Choose at least one of these helpful tips and then begin using it tomorrow morning (or even today, if you choose to exercise in the afternoon).
   - **Find a fitness partner.** Get in touch with another mom who will commit to exercising with you at least twice a week.
   - **Make exercise a family affair.** Go Rollerblading or biking with the kids, dance together after dinner, or go on a nature hike every week.
   - **Make exercise entertaining.** Listen to some tunes or a good audiobook while you go walking.

◉ **Don't just go by the scale.** Let your body be your guide and judge your fitness level by how you feel throughout the day or how well your clothes fit.

◉ **Reward yourself.** While you are working toward an ideal weight or body size, put a picture of an outfit you want in a place where you will see it throughout the day (like on the fridge). Buy the outfit when you reach your goal.

3. This is your day to focus on reducing or eliminating animal protein from your diet. Hopefully you've picked up some good vegetarian cookbooks from your library or bookstore. Try out some new recipes but remember that you can also improve on some of your family's favorite meals by replacing the meat with vegetarian substitutions. For example, try veggie sausage on your pizza or veggie chicken in your casserole.

House Rules

Managing a home and a family is not a job for those with weak stomachs. It gets downright dirty in the trenches, and you've only got two choices: Clean it up or surrender to the mess. And for your health, safety, and sanity, I would highly suggest the former. But keeping your home neat and clean does not mean you need to prance around in a frilly apron with a bottle of antibacterial spray in one hand and an electrostatic duster in the other. You can keep a clean house and still have a life. All you have to do is abide by some simple housekeeping rules.

House Rule #1: Develop a Structure

If you spend your days running from one fire to the next, you're likely to go up in smoke. Like every other endeavor, housework needs a plan of attack. Schedule some daily housekeeping tasks, whether it's vacuuming the carpet or scrubbing the tub. Doing a little bit every day can eliminate those all-day cleaning marathons, because dirt does not get a chance to accumulate. Try to get the housework done as early in the day as possible — maybe a thirty-minute cleaning "block" — so that you can get it over with and enjoy your day. You can also chip away at heavy-duty cleaning projects in a zone by scheduling your cleaning in blocks of time spread out over the entire week.

House Rule #2: Clean When It's Dirty

Many people ask me how often they should perform certain cleaning routines, such as changing the linens or cleaning the windows. The answer to this question is simple: Do it when it gets dirty. The woman with two kids at school all day does not need to vacuum as often as I do, with seven kids home all day long. It all comes down to your personal tolerance level and the rate at which your home gets dirty. You have enough to do without adding unnecessary cleaning to the list. Figure out how often your home gets dirty and clean accordingly.

Cleaning for cleaning's sake is just pointless. Do what needs to be done. Cleaning is supposed to set the stage for life; it's not the actual performance. You've got a life to live and dreams to follow, so if it's not dusty, don't dust it. If it's not dirty, don't wash it. And this applies to laundry as well. Kids can wear their pajamas more than one night.

> "My second favorite household chore is ironing. My first being hitting my head on the top bunk bed until I faint."
> —ERMA BOMBECK

GREEN CLEANING

Save your health and the planet by using ecologically friendly cleaners. As the watchdog for the health of your family, you shouldn't allow anything that could be potentially dangerous to touch the surfaces in your home or leave molecules in the air, especially if you have little ones running around. Their systems are much more sensitive to chemicals in the environment. Some of the friendliest cleaners are probably right there in your kitchen, so try these simple recipes:

- **Child-safe all-purpose cleaner:** 1/8 cup baking soda and 2 cups water

Your husband can use the same towel for several showers. And unless your jeans have baby spit-up on them (which around my house is highly likely), you can wear them a few days in a row. Make as little work for yourself as possible.

House Rule #3: Hide the Evidence

This is one of my favorite rules. With little items all over the house, things can get cluttered and messy quite quickly. Buy cabinets with doors, chests with drawers, and solid baskets and bins in order to corral all of the stuff. Open shelves and transparent boxes do nothing to hide the mess. If you can hide the clutter, your house will look much neater and more organized (even if it isn't). Clean is 10 percent perspiration and 90 percent perception. If it looks clean, then that's usually good enough.

Hiding stuff away in bins and boxes is great, but make sure you label everything so that it can stay organized. Then when that cleaning zone comes around on your calendar, you can go through all the containers

- **All-purpose cleaner:** 1/4 teaspoon liquid dish detergent or liquid Castile soap and 2 cups water
- **Abrasive powder:** baking soda
- **Acidic cleaner** (for soap scum and mineral deposits): 1 part vinegar, 1 part water
- **Disinfecting cleaner:** 1/4 teaspoon liquid dish detergent, 2 cups water, 4 tablespoons bleach
- **Glass cleaner:** 1/2 cup isopropyl alcohol, 1/2 cup water, 4 tablespoons ammonia
- **Furniture polish:** 1/2 cup vinegar, 1/2 cup light olive oil, 2 tablespoons lemon oil (or scent with essential oil)—spray, then buff thoroughly with a dry cloth

and tidy up a bit (like getting all of the Polly Pockets out of the Lego box or making sure the kids aren't using your sewing bin as a trash can).

House Rule #4: Practice the Art of Camouflage

Get smart and design your way out of housework. After all, your kids don't need the stress of keeping everything sparkling clean, and neither do you. You live in a home, not a museum. Go for fabrics and carpets that resist dirt or have a pattern that hides it easily. Avoid white at all costs in your decorating (unless you're talking about fabrics that can be bleached to death). And incorporate pattern and color on the bottom four feet of every wall in the house, (for example, use decorative wallpaper underneath a chair rail.) Children are all artists inside, and they will eventually color on the walls (or worse). The more you can hide, the less you have to clean.

House Rule #5: Set an Ultimatum

Desperate times call for desperate measures. If you are having difficulty staying on top of your housekeeping, invite someone over. Planning a dinner party or a luncheon will make you get off your fanny and get out the vacuum. Go ahead and indulge your inner socialite by hosting a guest or two, or twelve. Your home will sparkle, and you will

TOTAL MOM TIP
Time It!

Pick up an inexpensive egg timer and use it to put some pepper in your step. Set it for fifteen minutes and then attack the bathroom (you'll be surprised at how quickly you can accomplish the task when you are being timed). You can also time yourself on other repetitive tasks to see how quickly you can get them done. And it works well to motivate the kids, too.

be the one to accomplish all of the housework. Not because you want to but because you have to. Hey, it works.

House Rule #6: Foster Habits of Completion

Begin developing habits of completion that will carry you above and beyond your housework. Much of the work around the house is created by our normal living pattern. We tend to take the shortest route to achieve the final goal, and in the process, we mess up our homes. Focus on completing everything you do without allowing any rest stops. For example, when you unwrap something, don't leave the trash on the counter — throw it in the garbage. When you take off your jacket, don't throw it on the sofa — hang it up. When you finish reading, don't toss the book on the floor — put it back on the shelf. When a pen doesn't work don't put it back in the drawer — toss it in the trash.

These little habits of completion will help you keep your head above water. If you spend more energy on simple maintenance, then the majority of the work takes care of itself. Just keep repeating to yourself, "Don't put it down. Put it away." This mantra will help you reach your target without the usual rest stops that drag you down later.

TOTAL MOM TIP
The
Mat Method

The best way to get rid of the dirt in your house is to keep it outside where it belongs. Large Astroturf mats are God's gift to homemakers because they are awesome at scraping dirt off shoes. And believe me, I have tried my fair share of mats. Get the largest ones possible and place them outside every door in your home. They come in all colors, so you don't have settle for the green ones with fake daisies in the corner. And maintenance is a cinch. Every once in a while, pick up the mats, stand amazed at the dirt that collects underneath them, then sweep off the entrance and hose off the mats.

House Rule #7: Enlist the Troops

You are managing a family, and one aspect of that is enabling your children to become responsible individuals. When you do everything for your kids, you are encouraging their dependence and fostering laziness. Help yourself as well as your children by sharing the responsibilities around the house. Even the youngest children can learn how to pick up toys or put dirty laundry in a basket. And the days of gender stereotypes are long gone. Teach your girls home and car repair (they will thank you later) and teach your boys how to cook and clean (your daughters-in-law will thank you later).

You are part of a family. Trying to pull the entire load yourself is exhausting and will eventually drive you to resentment and frustration. If you are beating your head against a wall trying to get your kids to help out more around the house, then try these two no-fail methods. One, make them earn their privileges; and two, reward them for their efforts.

These methods may seem a bit too commonsensical, but I have come across many moms who do not employ them. I have often heard women gripe about their kids not cleaning their room or not doing their homework because they spend all their time on a computer or game system. But the last time I checked, it was supposed to be work before play. Children (of all ages) need to learn that privileges are earned. If they don't learn this early on, then they'll have a whole host of problems later on in life.

Help your children develop an appreciation for the rewards that come with hard work. When they do a good job, be generous with the praise, the privileges, and the prizes. Compliment them on their work and let them enjoy *earning* the fringe benefits that come along with being a kid—the toys, games, chats, etc. Instead of allowance, give earnings. Kids, especially older ones, can benefit from earning their own money and learning money management skills to go along with it. It's a win-

win scenario. It takes effort and time, but none of us chose motherhood for the ease and comfort, did we?

Week Three, Day Five: Daily Exercises

1. Today you are going to develop a chore chart to plot out your housework throughout the week. In your journal, write down all the tasks that you have to do on a weekly basis. Take a mental trip through your home and list everything that needs to be done in order for it to be neat and clean. Now print out a downloadable chore chart from the Total Mom Web site or just get a sheet of paper and list the days of the week across the top, Monday through Sunday. Divide the tasks that you listed among the days and make sure you coordinate the tasks to coincide with any regular routines. For example, I collect the trash on Monday because the garbage collector comes on Tuesday. I also clean the bathrooms on Friday because my kids often have guests sleep over on the weekends. Now you have a game plan! Post your completed chart in a place where you will see, it throughout the day. Make your chore chart today but don't try to begin the chores until Monday so you have some time to prepare for it. See my chore chart on the next page:

2. If your kids are old enough, make out a chore chart for them as well. Include in it a place for them to check off their work with a pencil, a stamp, or even a little foil star. Remember to give them incentive to complete their work by establishing the amount they get paid or the privileges that they earn. Be sure to include your children in developing this chart and clarify exactly what is expected so there is no confusion.

3. This is your day to cut back on processed foods. Spend plenty of time browsing through the produce department of your local grocery

store or make a visit to your local farmer's market and pick up plenty of fruits and vegetables for meals and snacks in between. This can be an exciting adventure to share with your kids and, an opportunity to introduce them to some new varieties.

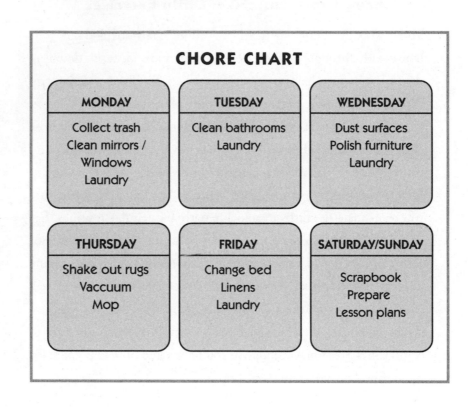

CHORE CHART

MONDAY	TUESDAY	WEDNESDAY
Collect trash Clean mirrors / Windows Laundry	Clean bathrooms Laundry	Dust surfaces Polish furniture Laundry

THURSDAY	FRIDAY	SATURDAY/SUNDAY
Shake out rugs Vaccuum Mop	Change bed Linens Laundry	Scrapbook Prepare Lesson plans

WEEK THREE

Weekend Workout

Home: If you don't already have one, pick up a caddy this weekend to store your cleaning supplies. If you have all of your tools together, it will cut the time it takes to do your daily cleaning tasks. If you have a large house, you may need two or three to store supplies under the sinks or in linen closets. If you want to make your own cleaners, drop by a beauty supply store and pick up some cute spray bottles to label and store your homemade cleaners, or just use some that you already have around the house. If you want to use essential oils, you can usually find them at a natural foods store. This is the weekend to begin de-cluttering Zone 2. Remember to reward your efforts — maybe a new candle for the room, some matching hangers for the closet, or just a good book and a cup of tea.

Health: Remember to keep that B.A.D. C.R.A.P. out of your diet! Win the family over to a healthy lifestyle by making some treats for them this weekend, maybe some oatmeal cookies with whole wheat flour or some delicious black bean brownies (get the recipe from TotalMom. com). You should also be getting some daily exercise. Try increasing your F.I.T. level by adding some hand weights to your walk or adding a few more minutes to your routine. If you are trying to get in shape, then take a moment to record your weight and the measurements around your waist, hips, and each thigh. Date this in your journal so that you can look back and compare. You can even get a friend to take a picture of you to put in your journal as a "before" shot.

Family: On Day Three you created a behavior chart to help your children develop responsibility. Along with this, you can use some downloadable monthly planner sheets from TotalMom.com or an inexpensive calendar; allow your children to put a stamp or sticker on each day they performed well. You can also help educate your children about finances by letting them help you shop. See if they can come up with clever ways to save money — buy generic instead of name brand? Buy larger packages for a smaller unit price? Use something you already have at home instead of buying new? Make it a game, and they will gladly play along!

Life: Keep asking yourself, "What do I *really* want?" When you are tempted to watch junk, eat junk, think junk, or speak junk, remind yourself that your decisions today will determine your reality tomorrow. And don't let fear stand in the way of achieving your dreams. Keep taking little steps to approach your fears and deal with them in a healthy way. Your AM routine is a great time to deal with your fears by releasing them to God through prayer.

Congratulations!

You are halfway there! You have met your basic needs, and now you are conquering the insecurity and chaos that creep into the lives of so many moms. Now it's time to move on to Week Four and meet those love and relationship needs that will enrich your life in beautiful and amazing ways.

NURTURED MOM

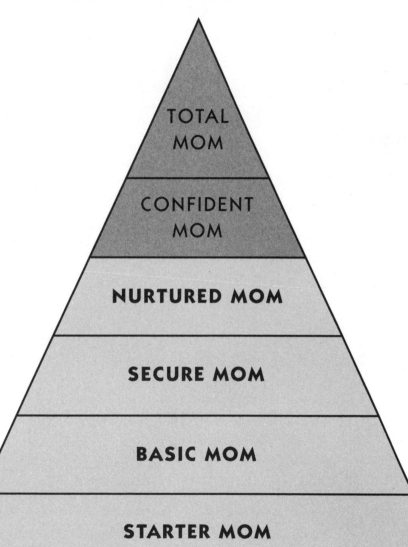

TOTAL
MOM

CONFIDENT
MOM

NURTURED MOM

SECURE MOM

BASIC MOM

STARTER MOM

The Sisterhood of the Total Moms

The nurtured mom is able to meet the needs of those around her. She can reach out to others and fully engage in her world. She can pour out her love and energy to the world around her because her tank is full and her heart is overflowing. No mom is an island. There is a world out there that can be fuller, richer, and better simply because you are a part of it. So don't hold back.

Gotta Have Girlfriends

Where would we be without our girlfriends? They help us figure out when to toilet train our kids, how to wear our jeans, and what to do in bed with our husbands. They are a wellspring of support, and we need them. But, if you are like me, the demands of life can creep up on you, and before you know it, your friends get shoved off the calendar. Many moms are guilty of giving, giving, giving, without stopping once in a while to receive. Before long, our tanks are empty and our nerves are raw. You can't let this happen. You need your friends for enrichment, encouragement, and accountability. And your friends need you as well. You have a lot to offer this world, and it begins with that circle of people around you. If you pull yourself away from a support network of other women, then it's not just you who misses out. There may be a mom out there who will never get to experience the blessing of knowing you or reap the benefits of your insight and wisdom. So get out there and start growing your garden of girlfriends.

Grow Your Garden

For many women, becoming a mom translates into going into hiding for a few months (or years) until life becomes manageable once more. But manageability is pretty subjective. Before too long, simply trying to make it through the day is your accepted way of life. You get accustomed to coping alone instead of giving and receiving support. And support is something that all moms, especially new moms, desperately need.

Give yourself plenty of time to adjust to maternal demands but don't wait for things to get back to normal before connecting with your friends, because things will never get back to normal. With motherhood, there are always a million things to do, minor emergencies to handle, and challenges to face. If your friends are moms, then they understand that sometimes the house is messy or your hair isn't washed. Go ahead and welcome them into your crazy and often disheveled world.

But it's up to you to get out there and start growing your garden of friends. Keep in contact with your friends and make sure you schedule dates to get together, even if things are hectic around the house. You don't need to throw a big spring fling and call the caterer. All you really have to do is pick up the phone or send an e-mail. Maybe you can invite some friends to meet you and the kids at a park somewhere. Or, if the weather is keeping you inside, see if some friends would like to come over and make cookies (they can all take some home afterward). But do it now. You need your friends, and your friends need you.

Project: Friendship

You've heard the saying "Many hands make light work." But many hands also make the work a lot more fun. Moms constantly have projects up their sleeves. A good way to foster friendships and get your work done at the same time is to include your friends in some of your projects. You will all reap the benefits of quality time together and successful work accomplished. And if you have kids of the same age, they can enjoy a playdate as well. Here are some ideas to get you started:

- Everyone can stock up the freezer with meals by spending one day cooking together. Plan some recipes that everyone likes; then assign ingredients to each individual who participates (enough for everyone). Each mom arrives with ingredients and cookware in hand, and leaves with some casseroles, cookies, or other delicacies that she can stock in the freezer for a later date.

- Ask a friend to come over for a particularly challenging project. Are you trying to de-clutter your closet but having a difficult time knowing what to keep and what to toss? A real friend will tell you which clothes look better in the trash can than on your body.

- Holidays can be a bit hectic. Invite some friends over to make gifts together (especially gifts for neighbors or teachers). Check out some seasonal craft magazines for good handmade gift ideas and let everyone agree on something. Each person can bring supplies, and everyone can make the crafts together. You can even do a cookie exchange where each person brings one type of cookie and then everyone exchanges their cookies so that you go home with a wide assortment of goodies.

- Give those green thumbs a workout by helping one another out with gardening or yard work. Take turns spending a morning or afternoon at one another's houses helping with the weeding, trimming, and planting. The kids can play outside while you work.

Keep It Real

If there is one thing I can't stand, it's pretentiousness. It ranks right up there with Brussels sprouts, mosquitoes, and control-top pantyhose. Please, please, *puh-leeze* don't fall into the trap of pretentiousness. Real friends love you for who you are, not for who you *think* you are. That's the wonderful thing about friendship. You just throw it all out there and see what sticks. Trying to be something you are not is a result of not believing in yourself. You will only be able to foster true friendships when you get to the point in life where you can truly accept yourself.

Forget about trying to be the perfect person or even the right person. Neither one exists. Are you worried you don't have enough money? You aren't the right size? You don't live in the right part of town or in the right house? Forget it! These images that we force upon ourselves don't just define us, they restrict us. Thankfully, you are more than a home or a dress size. You are a unique individual who has a lot to offer the world. Be you, because no one on earth is better qualified. And if by chance you are judged negatively, then you wouldn't want that person for a friend anyway. But don't do yourself or anyone else a disservice by being someone you are not. You and your friends deserve the real you.

> "It is one of the blessings of old friends that you can afford to be stupid with them."
> —RALPH WALDO EMERSON

Talkin' Trash

If there is one sure way to poison your crop of friends, it's through gossip. Although it may appear benign, gossip is actually toxic to everyone involved. It hurts the people being talked about because they are not there to offer their opinions or defend themselves, and it hurts the people who are doing the talking because they are allowing negative thoughts and images to creep up and take control. Gossip accomplishes nothing. It is just a lazy and hurtful way to try to make yourself look better by making someone else look worse.

When you feel as if you are surrounded by discouragement, gossip, and bitterness, it's up to you to come up with ways to creatively steer the discussion and the person toward a more positive frame of mind. Try to change the course of the discussion, bring up some good news, or compliment the person speaking (or the person being gossiped about). You may just be the only ray of sunshine that some people will have in their gray and cloudy days. Don't shut off the people; just shut off the negativity.

Don't Love Them the Most

Friends are extremely important, but never as important as family. There are some chapters in life when you have to choose between the two, like when all your girlfriends are getting together to play cards, but your family hasn't had a sit-down dinner in two weeks. Or when your girlfriends are going shopping on the evening of the day your husband returns home from a business trip. Sometimes it's easier to choose friends over family, but life isn't always about making the easier choice. It's about making the choice that yields the highest return. If you want family to last, then it takes work and a little sacrifice here and there. If your friends are truly your friends, then they will understand and even encourage you to invest in your family first. Love your friends and make time for them in your life, but never choose them over your family.

While this is an important rule of thumb, sometimes you just need to vent. I understand. If you're going to complain about your husband or your kids, only do so to a friend who you know will encourage you to improve the situation and help you come up with creative solutions. If your friend aggravates the situation by putting more steam in your engine, then you're better off not complaining at all. Watch your words because they become your actions. And watch your friends because they often determine your words. You want a support network, not a lynch mob.

You don't have to plan a big, fat, knockdown, drag-out social scene just to get together with friends. Sometimes spontaneity is best. I have a close friend who has kids the same age as some of mine. Every now and then an e-mail will come through from her that simply says, "Can the Keeley family come out and play?" I throw the kids in the van and meet her at the park. Try to add more spontaneity to your life when it comes to your girlfriends. Call completely out of the blue and invite some friends over for a movie, or maybe swing by a friend's house and drop off that extra pie you made. All it takes is a little effort, but it yields enormous results.

Weed Your Garden

Sometimes you just need to create some room in your garden. There are weeds that pop up every now and then. If you don't pull them out, they can ruin your entire crop and become a disastrous headache for you. This may sound a bit harsh, but you should pour your energy into only those relationships that bring out the best in you. If you have friends who are constant complainers, negative thinkers, or bitter individuals, by all means, try to change them. But remember, it is not your job to change them. It's only your job to change yourself and how you respond to them. If your efforts aren't making a dent, then you may be better off distancing yourself.

Sometimes you have to weed the garden. Ask yourself some questions about your friends. "Do they want the best *for* me?" "Do they bring out the best *in* me?" Give it some serious thought because your friends can drag you down or push you to greatness. Choose them wisely because, in many ways, you become them. Don't feel guilty if in improving your life, you evolve out of certain relationships. This is inevitable. We all grow and change. And, hopefully, we improve our lives in the process.

You need friends. There's no question about that. You need them, and they need you. Even during those times in life when you want to pull away from the world and hibernate for a while, you still have the need inside for a network of friends. Don't let this need go unfulfilled. Friends are like mirrors—good ones will reflect our best selves.

Week Four, Day One: Daily Exercises

1. Each of your close friends nurtures different parts of your personality. One may bring you laughter; another may bring you wisdom. Grab that journal and write down the names of at least two friends who bring out the absolute best in you. Next to their names, write down the particular gifts they bring to your life. Now, today, write a thank-you note to each of these beautiful people and thank them for blessing your life. If you can't think of at least two friends who enrich your life, then take some productive steps this week to enlarge your social circle. Join a book club or church group. Look up chapters of mom groups in your area and get involved *this week*. Some good groups to begin with are MOPS (Mothers of Preschoolers) and MOMS club.

2. Think of a project that you can do more effectively and joyfully with friends by your side. It could be some marathon cooking or a multifamily yard sale, but find a project and call up some friends to join in. Set the date and put it on the calendar so you don't let it slip by.

3. Remember that this is the week you are de-cluttering Zone 2. It should already be written on Monday of your calendar. And practice House Rule #1: Develop a Structure by getting to those daily tasks that you scheduled for today on your chore chart.

Family Legacy

> "We spend most
> of our time and
> energy in a kind of
> horizontal thinking.
> We move along
> the surface of
> things . . . but there
> are times when we
> stop. We sit still. We
> lose ourselves in a
> pile of leaves or its
> memory. We listen
> and breezes from a
> whole other world
> begin to whisper."
> — JAMES CARROLL,
> *O MAGAZINE*

I believe that one of the best gifts we can give our children is a sense of legacy, a belief that there is a momentum, an energy, that precedes them, grounds them, and drives them forward. The moments that we spend together as a family give our children the gift of identity, the ability to understand who they are and where they belong in this continuously fluctuating world. Family events and celebrations, even the simple ones such as birthday parties or campfire sing-alongs, not only mark our passage through time but, in many ways, pave the path into the future. You can nurture your child by providing a firm family foundation to grow on. And this foundation grows from the moments, both big and small, planned and unplanned, that we spend together as a family. Those times when we retreat from the world and draw together as a unit are often the moments when we do most of our growing and learning.

In the Moment

Part of appreciating our passage through life is learning how to truly live in the moment. Our memories comprise a series of moments, those still frames in life when time is suspended and we are wrapped up in the present. If you are constantly preparing and planning for the future or stressing over and reviewing the past, then you are going to miss out on the greatest gift of all—the present. Existing in the here and now is often extremely difficult to do, especially for moms, who have a million and one things going on at any particular moment. You can be right in the middle of your son's fifth birthday party and catch yourself wondering if you should make an appointment next week to get your roots touched up. Before you know it, the memories that could have been stored in your heart have scattered and dissipated into thin air.

Living requires focus. If you are having a tea party with your little girl, then be completely there, not off somewhere planning your grocery list. Pour the tea, add some honey, sip a little, talk about ponies and princesses, look into her eyes and see how they sparkle and glisten, look at how her hair brushes against her tiny ears. These are the moments that life is built on. Life is giving and taking. Give your full attention to the here and now, especially when it comes to your family, and you can take from life a full heart and a lifetime of relationships and memories. Appreciate the beauty of right now.

> **TOTAL MOM TIP**
> **Hourly Moments**
>
> You should already be wearing a wristwatch with an hourly alarm that you use as an attitude checkpoint. This was one of the tips in Week One, Day Five. Try adding one more personal checkpoint to your hourly alarm: Are you truly appreciating this moment and living it to the fullest? Now whenever your hourly alarm goes off, you need to check your *attitude*—is it powerful and positive? And check your *existence*—is it here and now?

Stop, Look, and Listen

It's not just important to stop, look, and listen when you are crossing the street. It's also important when you are raising a family. Events and celebrations cause us to pause for a moment and completely appreciate the gifts that surround us. Moms have a tendency to get so busy managing life that they forget to appreciate life.

Stop! "Busy, busy, busy" seems to be the mantra for motherhood. My friends see that I get a lot done in my life, and so they think that I'm the busiest woman on earth. Actually, I get a lot done so that I have the opportunity to pause and appreciate my family. Instead of doing things like watching television or surfing the Internet, I try to choose the most productive use of my time. I do the stuff I *have* to do so I have time to do the stuff I *want* to do. Get your work done and out of the way so that you have the opportunity to *stop,* especially when the moments arrive that are too beautiful to pass by. When your son wants to play a game of checkers, you can play. When your daughter wants you to watch a puppet show, you can watch fully and completely, without worrying about what needs to be done next.

Look! Special family moments give us an opportunity to *look,* deeply and clearly, at all that life wants to show us. We should take plenty of pictures and videos, but the real moments of life should be stored within. Open your eyes and take a deep look at life. Don't just glance here and there, because it passes much too quickly. Take the time to create a memory in your heart. I can't even begin to tell you how many hours I have spent holding my babies, watching them inhale and exhale, seeing the way their tiny lashes rest against their cheeks, their little fingers balled up in fists. You have to understand the preciousness and brevity of life to really appreciate life. And the older my children get, the more I realize that these moments together are a gift. Keep your eyes and your heart open and soak them up.

Listen! Blair once took the older kids to the library so I could stay home with the baby. The silence in the house was deafening. I thought I would appreciate a little calm and quiet, but it was as if the hum of life was turned off. After a while, I was happy to see the van pull up and the kids pile out. Special family moments help us tune in to the activity of life around us. It's important to remember that we can either *hear* or *listen*. You may *hear* your child ask if you can come outside and play Frisbee, but if you *listen,* you can understand that he wants to spend time with you and that you are the only one he wants to enjoy this gorgeous day with. You may *hear* your daughter complain about her friends, but if you *listen,* you will realize that she needs your help figuring out how to deal with people and navigate through new social situations. *Hearing* and *listening* are not the same thing. Make sure you are doing both.

Head and Heart

A family legacy is established through moments — those times in life when we pause to fully engage with those we love and drink it all in. As a mom, you are the chief historian of your family. It is up to you to create and collect these special moments, and it requires your head as well as your heart. Use your head to plan for celebrations, rituals, and other special events. I can tell you right now — if you don't plan it, it's not going to happen. Look for opportunities to mark life's events. There are always holidays and birthdays, but why not create your own traditions? Think of special days and special ways to celebrate. We always paint our faces for Mardi Gras, read Christmas stories every night throughout December, and enjoy "Family Movie Night" on Fridays. Get that head of yours going by creating some fun traditions that you can celebrate as a family.

Legacy is created through your heart, too. What family memories are you building in your children? Memories don't always happen when we schedule them. Sometimes you just have to follow your heart. It may be a perfectly beautiful day to enjoy the park. Even though you haven't scheduled it in your planner, why not throw sandwiches in a bag, kids in the car, and get out there and enjoy it? You may need to polish the furniture, but your daughter wants to play in the mud puddles. Why not challenge her to a mud-stomping contest? Don't limit those family moments to scheduled events. Let your heart pull you to places where some of the best memories are made.

TOTAL MOM TIP
Can the Clutch

Forget about little clutch bags when you go out (unless, of course, you are slinking down a red carpet). When you go out, carry a fairly large tote so that you have enough room to toss in a camera before you leave or throw in some memorabilia while you're out. Make it a habit of carrying a camera with you, even if it's just to the grocery store. You never know when that perfect photo op will present itself.

Stretch Those Creative Muscles

Our family is constantly celebrating something, whether it's a visit from the tooth fairy or a cookout in the yard. Here are some of our favorites, but get creative and come up with some clever celebrations that identify and reflect your family.

- **School Kickoff Cookout:** We have a cookout at the end of summer to mark the last weekend before the beginning of school.
- **Goof-Off Days:** Each child is allowed two days of excused school absence every year to do nothing but hang out with a parent, hit the town, and have an entire day of fun.
- **Girls/Guys Night Out:** Every once in a while, Blair will take the boys out on a date and I will take the girls out on a date. We have done everything from bowling to rock climbing to salon trips (girls only).
- **Spook Night:** This is one that I remember as a kid. We turn off all of the lights in the house. The kids hide in the dark, and Blair tries to find them with a flashlight.

Fun Family Friday: Every Friday night, the family does a fun activity together, such as watch movies or play board games.

Archive It!

It's not enough to enjoy moments together and take the pictures to prove it. Eventually, you need to get those pictures out of storage and into a scrapbook. My kids prefer looking at our family scrapbooks to reading any other books in the house. It's easy to see why — they are drinking in their family history.

You will never find any of my scrapbook pages in a craft magazine. I have friends who can archive with the best, complete with lace, buttons, vellum, stamps, and foil embossing. However, I take a lot of pictures (I guess because I have a lot of kids). If I put that much effort into scrapbooking, it would drive me crazy because I wouldn't have time for anything else. Instead, I have come up with a method of archiving to save my memories and save my sanity all at the same time.

Here's what you need:

2 file boxes with lids

14 expandable file folders

3-drawered desktop organizer

1 box of clear heavy-duty plastic sheet protectors

3-ring binder (with a clear front that you can customize)

Step One: Label twelve file folders for the months of the year and place them in order in one of the file boxes. Label one of the remaining two file folders "Current" and place it at the front; label the other "Extras" and place it at the back.

Step Two: In the second file box, put $8^{1}/_{2} \times 11$ inch acid-free card stock paper that you will use for scrapbook pages. Get a wide variety of colors, including black and white. Put this paper in the file box in order of rainbow colors so that you can access it more easily (red, orange, yellow, green, blue, purple), with white, black, and neutral colors at the front.

Step Three: Place the box of sheet protectors in the back of the second file box.

Step Four: Load up the three-drawer organizer with some scrapbooking supplies. I keep markers in the top drawer, scissors in the middle drawer, and glue sticks in the bottom drawer. You may do a lot of stamping or embossing. If you do, then get another organizer to store those supplies.

Step Five: In the Extras file, put anything that you hold on to for scrapbooking purposes, like a book of quotes, stickers, or cute cartoons.

Step Six: Go through all of those stacks of pictures and file them away in the first file box according to the month they were taken. Digital pictures can be printed out and filed as well. If you are those then over a year behind on your pictures, make sure you label the envelope of pictures with the year that they were taken. If you collect things from specific events, like menus or cards, then place these in the appropriate month as well. Once you get all of your stuff filed, it will feel so good. This is a great way to make some progress on your archiving.

How to Scrapbook: All you need to do is start with the first month, glue the pictures to a page, slip the page into a sheet protector, and put it into the binder. However you want to label and embellish it is completely up to you. Personally, I like my pictures to have borders around them and a little bit of decoration on the page, like a quote, stickers, or funny speech balloons.

The important thing, though, is to get the pictures out of the enve-lopes and into a binder. Then you and the kids can enjoy looking back at all of the memories you have made (and the sheet protectors are especially good for those sticky little fingers).

If you are interrupted during your scrapbooking, all you need to do is stick the page that you are working on in the Current file and close up shop. No big mess to get out, no big mess to put away.

The Richness of Rituals

The awesome thing about your family's rituals is that they identify you as a singular, cohesive unit. Your family celebrations today will be the stories that your children tell your grandchildren tomorrow. Their fondest memories will be formed around the family, not around themselves. And these memories will be the ones that will not only entertain them in the future but sustain them as well.

One of my closest friends lost her mother at a relatively young age. It was painful for her to be without her mother as she was growing to be an adult, but she had beautiful memories to keep her going. She tells me of waking up on Christmas morning as a child to find a trail of red and green M&Ms from her bed to the Christmas tree, where an assortment of presents lay waiting for her. The light from her eyes tells me that this is a ritual that not only identified her as a part of a loving family but also consoled her during times of grief. When you are making time for special moments together, you are building a firm foundation for everyone in your family, a legacy that will sustain them through the good times as well as the bad.

Week Four, Day Two: Daily Exercises

1. In your journal, take a few minutes to write down the fondest family memories that you can recall. Did you celebrate any special holidays or rituals? Jot these special memories down and next to them write why they were so special. What exactly do you remember that was positive? I can still feel the goose bumps running down my spine whenever my dad would tell ghost stories, and hear the giggling coming from my mom when we would go shopping and I would sample the most atrocious makeup I could find.

2. Go through the list of ideas on this day and think of a special ritual or celebration that you can instill in your family. Write it down on the calendar and tell the kids about it so that they can share in the excitement—and don't forget the camera.

3. Practice House Rule #6: Foster Habits of Completion. Get to your chores early and do them completely so that you are free to enjoy the rest of the day with your family and cherish the moments that you have together.

Connect with Your Kitchen

The average American kitchen is being used for just about everything today except turning out wholesome, healthy family meals. It's a study hall, home office, coffee shop, even a fast-food dispensing unit. But it should be so much more than that. Our kitchens are the hearts of our homes, and they set the pace for all of the other activities that occur within our walls. If we can get the kitchen right, then the rest of the house flows along the same path. Whenever I start cleaning house, I always start with the kitchen. And if you are working on family unity, good health, and a nurturing home, these all start in the kitchen as well.

Personal Therapy

If you don't already have one, you need to foster a good, healthy relationship with your kitchen. Consider it your personal therapist. Your kitchen is the room where restoration and nourishment take place, for your body, mind, and spirit. In this hallowed room, you can discover new foods and prepare dishes that nourish those you love best. You can ground yourself and center your home. You can open up, sit back, and relax.

The kitchen can and will satisfy on so many levels, but it will only

> "Cooking is at once child's play and adult joy. And cooking done with care is an act of love."
> — CRAIG CLAIBORNE

give back to you what you put in to it. Take time every day to make your kitchen a nurturing spot. Light a candle, put out a dish of nuts, pick some flowers and put them beside a window. These little steps will make your kitchen a welcome and enriching spot to be. Your home needs this spot of therapy — for you and the rest of your family. Make your kitchen a room that you long to be in.

TOTAL MOM TIP
Only the Best

Make sure that your kitchen contains the best items your budget can afford so that you will feel inspired to get in there and prepare some healthy meals. If you have a hodgepodge of inferior plates, cups, and saucers, then consider giving them away and purchasing some new dishes. Plain white is always a good investment because it goes with everything and you can dress it up or down. If you have a ton of mismatched forks, spoons, and knives, then dump it all and invest in some heavy, durable flatware. It's better to have less of the best than lots of the junk. A restaurant supply company is a great source for high-quality dinnerware at a fraction of the price.

Dine Together

I know that life can be hectic at times. Between practice, games, meetings, work, and who knows what else, you often feel as if you are running a stop-and-go station instead of managing a home. But it is vital that you take the time to pause for a moment and regroup as a family. We need moments of unity to strengthen those cords that bind us together. Meals provide this opportunity. In eating together we not only feed our bodies, we also feed our souls. Food can nourish and energize, and so can unrushed time with those we love.

So take time to connect with your kitchen and feed your family. Free up several evenings every week in the family schedule to do nothing but eat, drink, and linger for a while around the dinner table. Even if you prepare something as simple as a pot of soup and a loaf of bread, the effort that you put in to feeding your family will reward you in amazing ways, body and soul!

TOTAL MOM TIP
Eat, Drink, and Be Merry

Have a reason for the family to hang around the dinner table instead of rushing off to do their own things. You could let everyone take turns sharing their happiest or funniest memories, telling the best thing that happened that day, or sharing what they want to be or do. Make it a bit more formal by playing a game, such as Twenty Questions," or asking trivia questions (a favorite around our dinner table). *The Kids' Book of Questions* by Gregory Stock is a great resource to spark some stimulating conversation around the dinner table.

Plan for Success

If you want something, you've got to plan for it. Otherwise, it's just another good idea that gets pushed on to the back burner and eventually gets lost somewhere behind the stove with the Legos. So if you want to connect with your kitchen and make mealtime a family affair, then you've got to plan it out. When you schedule your monthly meals (as you did in Week Two, Day Five), get the family involved. Get some suggestions from the kids to make sure that everyone's happy and throw a few new dishes on the calendar as well. And make sure you schedule some low-maintenance meals. I always mark a few days on our meal calendar as "**YO YO.**" We all eat together, but **Y**ou're **O**n **Y**our **O**wn when it comes to your meal! It's not important to have elaborate meals. What *is* important is that you are eating healthy meals together as a family.

TOTAL MOM TIP
Leftover
Success

Leftovers don't have to be boring. Whenever I need to clear out some leftovers, I let one of the children make a menu and take orders. I always list entrées on one side and side dishes on the other, and let them pick one of each. If they are lucky, dessert choices are thrown in there as well. The combinations can get pretty strange, but it's a surefire way to clean out the fridge. Let your kids have fun with this. They can even illustrate the menus or put on an apron and a chef's hat to take orders in style.

Stock Your Pantry

It's important to keep a well-stocked pantry. I wasn't always great about staying on top of my supplies. There was always a last-minute run to the store for something. Finally, I came up with a great way to keep groceries and other household supplies well stocked. I created a master list of all of the categories of a typical grocery store, made copies, and posted one of them on my refrigerator. It became my grocery list. When I run out of something, I put it on the list under that category. When I plan out my meals, I put the items I need on the list as well. It helps me keep up with my supplies as well as save a lot of time when I am shopping. I don't have to scan the entire list when I go down an aisle, just that one category.

Sneaky Nutrition

Part of being a good mom is being a sneaky mom, and that definitely applies to nutrition. This week, begin using your creativity to invent ways of sneaking healthy food into your kids' diets. For example, I add flax meal to my whole-grain brownies (chocolate can disguise almost anything). I sprinkle toasted wheat germ on their soy ice cream. I take carrots,

PANTRY PLANNER

You can write down the categories below and create a Pantry Planner, or download a Pantry Planner from the TotalMom Web site. Print it out, post it in your kitchen, and you can easily stay on top of all of your supplies.

- Herbs, Spices, Seasonings
- Rice, Boxed Meals, Side Dishes
- Meat or Meat Replacements
- Household Supplies
- Baking Items
- Dairy and Refrigerated Items
- Health, Family, Personal Items
- Grains, Breads, Pastas
- Beverages
- Canned and Packaged Goods
- Snacks
- Frozen Items
- Fruits and Vegetables
- Condiments, Sauces, Spreads
- Miscellaneous Items

mushrooms, and sea vegetables, chop them up beyond recognition, and add them to stews. I shower their popcorn with nutritional yeast. I even use soy cheese and whole wheat noodles in their macaroni and cheese. Stealth health is the best health as far as kids are concerned because they have no idea they are actually eating food that is good for them.

Three Sneaky Steps

When it comes to increasing the nutritional quality of your family's diet, think in terms of the three S's:

Subtract — You already began your journey toward eliminating the unhealthy food from your family's diet. Your kids may not have even noticed that there hasn't been bologna in the house for more than a week or that their Kool-Aid has magically disappeared.

Substitute — Think of things they normally eat that you can replace with healthier alternatives. Can you substitute whole wheat pasta for the enriched stuff? How about replacing that sugary jelly with some 100 percent fruit spread?

Supplement — This is my favorite sneaky method. I add a bit of stuff here and there, and they hardly ever notice. The best dishes to add power-packed nutrition to are soups, stews, sauces, pastas, and baked dishes and desserts.

Here are some ideas to get your creativity in high gear:

- Replace some of the oil in a cake, cookie, or bread recipe with prune puree.
- Add powdered sea kelp (yes, sea kelp), chopped cremini mushrooms, or Grape-Nuts to spaghetti sauce.
- Sprinkle flax meal and toasted wheat germ on oatmeal.
- Add millet or quinoa grain to stews and soups.
- Replace some of the eggs in egg salad with firm tofu.

Plan, Prepare, Pause

It doesn't take a lot of time or energy to feed your family. The important things are to plan, prepare, and pause. *Plan* your meals out so that you don't need to break a sweat when dinnertime approaches. *Prepare* for your meals by keeping your pantry well stocked. And take the time to *pause*. When the sunlight begins to cast long shadows and our hunger begins to creep in, it's nice to know that a healthy meal around the family dinner table awaits us. And as generations have done before us, we will gather together with those we love best to nourish every aspect of our being. Yes, connecting with your kitchen is very important, for you and for your family.

Week Four, Day Three: Daily Exercises

1. In your journal, write down some ideas to persuade your family to gather around the dinner table. Make a favorite dessert, plan out some favorite family meals, or get them to linger a bit by playing a game during the meal. Make sure you follow through with your ideas. Why not play a round of Twenty Questions or I Spy this evening?

2. Go through your recipe collection and find four or more recipes that you can alter with the three S's of sneaky. Write down some new versions of these recipes and plan to try out at least two of them this week. Be patient. I have cooked up some major disappointments, but by and large, my efforts to give a recipe a healthy makeover have been extremely successful.

3. Practice House Rule #7: Enlist the Troops by getting the whole family involved. Get some easy recipes (children's cookbooks are great sources) and let the kids do the chopping, stirring, and setting the table. They can also make the kitchen a pleasant place to hang out by picking some flowers for a centerpiece.

Home, Sensual Home

> "There is nothing like staying at home for real comfort."
> — JANE AUSTEN, *EMMA*

When your senses are satisfied, all is right with the world. Nothing much can bother me when I'm sipping on a mango smoothie at an outdoor beach café with a warm jasmine-scented breeze in the air and the sound of a street-side jazz band playing in the background. All of my senses are stimulated and fulfilled, and it is pure heaven!

Your home should be pure heaven. If you find yourself thinking that it probably ranks down there with purgatory or lower, then it's up to you to make some changes. It doesn't matter whether your home is six hundred square feet or six thousand square feet. The important thing is that it is a source of inspiration and rejuvenation. Your heart should feel warmer and your load lighter the minute you step inside. Getting rid of the clutter sets the stage. Cleaning it up gets it in motion. But the time and energy that you put into beautifying your home will reward you in so many ways. And the best way to spread beauty throughout your home is by appealing to the senses — sight, sound, smell, touch, and taste.

Sight for Sore Eyes

No matter how beautiful your home is, if it is cluttered and messy, then that's what it's going to look like — cluttered and messy. The first step to making your home visually appealing is to create a sense of space. As you continue to de-clutter your home, you will find that the feeling of openness is both energizing and peaceful at the same time. Display only what you consider to be truly beautiful or necessary and keep the rest out of the way.

Color is also very important in creating a visually nurturing space. Don't be afraid to add some to your home. Many people are reluctant to experiment with color in their homes because they are worried about getting that perfect shade. Go ahead and venture out a bit and swipe on a hue that reflects you. If you are absolutely clueless as to where to begin when adding color to your home, then just find one thing you love — a painting, a mug, a fabric, anything — and pull colors from that to use throughout your home.

> **TOTAL MOM TIP**
> **Mix Things Up**
>
> Breathe some fresh life into your home by moving the furniture or decorations around. As you are de-cluttering Zone 2 this week, try switching things around a bit until it feels right. Maybe it's time to switch out that painting for an antique mirror or move that lamp to a different spot. Mixing things up a bit makes the whole zone feel new and fresh.

Experimenting with patterns is another way of creating visual beauty. A home can get pretty boring if you don't mix things up a bit, so try some mixing and matching with different patterns and designs. A common rule of thumb is if you stay in the same color family, you can mix up patterns, such as throwing in pink stripes with pink florals. But rules were made to be broken, so if something just screams your name, then display it. If you stick with what you truly love, then you can't go wrong.

Listen Up

The sounds of home are so beautiful. I think the sweetest sound that we could ever surround ourselves with is the sound of life. A home isn't meant to stand empty and still. It is meant to be dynamic and exciting, a safe place where we can fail and succeed, where we can create new things and make plenty of mistakes along the way. Life isn't meant to be perfect. Life is meant to be lived, and when it comes to family life, silence means that there is no real living taking place. Noise? Now that means that something real is going on! Don't hush the noise, embrace it.

Music is another beautiful sound that all of us can incorporate into our homes. My own kids have always taken music lessons, even when we could barely make ends meet. The ability to appreciate, understand, and communicate music is one thing that I have always wanted my children to have. Let your kids take music lessons, even if it means buying a secondhand guitar and borrowing a self-teaching book or video. Learning to play an instrument is a gift that they will always have, even if they are too young to appreciate it now.

Music should also be an integral part of your interior design. Play your favorite music but don't get stuck in the same genre. Try out different tunes once in a while. We live in a world of diversity, and the more we

TOTAL MOM TIP
The
Family Playlist

My brother gave me an excellent idea that I must pass along. His family makes a playlist every few months, and then they play it whenever they are together, such as while they are in the car or hanging out at home. We started doing the same thing, and it has been so much fun. Every person gets to pick out one song for the list (smaller families can pick out two or three per person), and then we play that music when we are together. We do it every season and collect the playlists.

know, the more we want to find out. Music is the language that connects all of us, so try tuning in to something a little exotic. I was very fortunate to marry a man who had traveled throughout the world (before he had to settle down, grow some roots, and raise a bunch of kids). He opened my eyes to music from around the world, and now we try to do the same for our children.

The Nose Knows

Our olfactory sense is extremely powerful. One whiff of something familiar and memories come flooding back. I'm a big "smell" person. Everything in my home has to smell pleasant (which is extremely difficult when you have three boys sharing a bathroom!). It can be a pretty tough battle, but it's worth it.

There are a lot of effective ways to make your home smell nice, and you don't have to resort to chemicals to do it. I once used air fresheners like they were going out of style. I had one in almost every room, and they went nicely with the lingering headaches that I had developed. After reading about indoor air pollution and the health risks that can ensue, I got rid of the air fresheners and petroleum-based candles, and within days my headaches disappeared. A lot of the synthetic fragrances that we use in our homes, either to clean or to scent, emit dangerous, even carcinogenic molecules into the air that eventually end up in our lungs, bloodstream, and stored in our bodies. The air in our world is polluted enough without us contributing to it in our own homes. Make your home both aromatic and healthy by using safe and natural products. Here are some perfectly natural ways to scent your home:

- ◎ Delicious cooking is still a favorite. One homemade loaf of bread or a batch of cookies can scent your entire home.
- ◎ Soy candles smell great, and as an added benefit, they last a lot longer than their petroleum-based counterparts.
- ◎ After you peel an apple or an orange, put the peelings in a pot

with water, some cinnamon, and cloves and let it simmer (keep an eye on it). You can also sprinkle this mixture on a pan and stick it in a warm oven.

- ❂ Dab essential oils on lightbulb rings.
- ❂ Use essential oils to scent your homemade cleaners (see Week Three, Day Five) and wipe off surface areas or do a quick mopping.
- ❂ Odor is caused by bacteria; cleaning is the most effective way to get rid of it.

You've Got the Touch

If you have ever scraped two pieces of Styrofoam together, then you understand the importance of touch. Touch is such a beautiful sense to spread through your home. There's nothing I like more on a cold night than to cuddle up under a warm blanket. And when the temperature starts rising, I love the feel of sand under my feet and an ocean breeze on my skin. We should always find ways to indulge our sense of touch through our homes. From the time you wake up to the time you turn in at night, spoil yourself and those you love by making your surroundings absolutely touchable.

When you get dressed in the morning, make sure that your clothes don't just look good but feel good as well (and that includes your bra and underwear). If you're tugging and pulling at them all day, then you're not going to get a lot accomplished. And we all know that you have to get a LOT accomplished, so dress for it. This may be the best effort you can put into your home, because when you look good and feel good, you will get much more done around the house. And remember that you don't have to sacrifice fashion for comfort.

Communicate with touch through your interior design. Play up the textures in each room to encourage people to sit back and relax. Have some floor pillows handy for the kids to sit on and some cozy blankets to use for a quick snuggle. Balance your textures by juxtaposing rough fabrics with softer ones. I visited a friend once who had burlap curtains in the dining room with little delicate ribbons on them. The contrast was stunning and beautiful! Just go into a fabric store and follow your fingers. You never know what you could discover!

By far, the best way to celebrate the sense of touch in our homes is to touch one another. I grew up in the South, and we don't shake hands there, we hug! I remember coaching my husband on proper Southern etiquette when he was about to meet my family for the first time. "Now remember," I said. "Don't stick out your hand. That's rude. Spread out your arms instead." You don't have to be a Southern girl to appreciate the fine art of hugging and holding. Become more conscious of how often you pull your kids or your husband close to you. Hug them, hold them, and let your love be communicated through the sense of touch.

Good Taste

Yes, the sense of taste can be a perfectly pleasing part of your interior design. One sip of sweet tea or a bite of a buttermilk biscuit with a slice of homegrown tomato stuck in the middle and I am whisked back to my younger days. The sense of taste can create warm memories of home and family. And contrary to what many people believe, healthy food does not have to taste like grass and cardboard.

Don't skip dessert! Meals are satisfying, but dessert brings sweetness to life. You can often reduce the sugar in some of your favorite desserts and still create something delectable. I enjoy making batches of oatmeal cookies or the occasional berry cobbler, especially if I make it with healthy ingredients. As an added benefit, dessert is a great tool to bribe your kids to finish their vegetables!

The Sixth Sense

More information is communicated through your sixth sense than through all of your other senses combined. Your environment can look, taste, smell, sound, and feel great, but if you do not have a spirit of gratitude, something will feel a bit off. You bless your home in powerful ways when you first consider it a blessing to you and your family. Even if it is not your "dream home," begin right now to appreciate those walls that enclose you and the roof that keeps you sheltered. Forget about what your home lacks. If it is not as big as you would like, consider it a blessing for pulling your family closer together. If your home is not in an ideal area, consider it a blessing for allowing you to be a light in the darkness. Let your gratitude permeate every nook and cranny of where you live, and it will light up your home with beauty.

TOTAL MOM TIP
Create Some Ambience

Plan a few family dinners every month as theme meals. Pick a different culture and plan a meal around it, complete with theme music. You can download the music from the Internet or check out the CDs at Putumayo.com, a company that specializes in kid-friendly music from other cultures—these are some of our family favorites. Pasta tastes so much better with our *Italian Café* CD playing in the background.

Week Four, Day Four: Daily Exercises

1. Take some time to consider how to use all five senses (sight, sound, smell, touch, and taste) to spread beauty through your home. In your journal, write down every room in your house on the left side of the paper and leave plenty of space between them. Next to each room, list some ways to beautify it sensually. For example, in the living

room you could get a throw blanket for the back of the couch, light a scented soy candle to put on the mantel, put out a dish of nuts, or get a trickling water fountain for a tabletop decoration. Pick out a few ideas and take some time today to add these touches of beauty throughout your home.

2. Take a gratitude walk through your home today. I do this every once in a while to help nurture an attitude of gratitude. Start at the front door and slowly walk throughout your house, into each and every room. As you walk, visualize all of the ways that your home nurtures you and your family and let thankfulness grow in your spirit. At the front door, you may visualize all of the wonderful people who have graced that area, all of the times your children have entered with smiles and excitement. You can even be thankful for those shoes scattered by the door, thankful for how they protect little feet and encourage bold steps into an unknown world. Your gratitude will grow as you walk through each room. Make a habit of doing this often, perhaps even every morning as you do your daily chores. This is a wonderful way to beautify your home and your spirit.

3. Practice House Rule #3: Hide the Evidence by designating a junk drawer in your kitchen. When you are rushed to clean up your kitchen, you can throw the occasional misplaced item in the drawer and get to it when the week arrives to deep clean and de-clutter the kitchen zone of your home.

Lovers' Talk

When we first get married, lovers' talk consists of oohing and aahing over future plans, sparkling eyes, and supple thighs (yours, not his). But as our marriages evolve, the giddy affection grows deeper and more forceful, like a rippling stream running into an ocean. We must learn to adjust ourselves and encourage this growth—increasing the depth of our relationship while holding on to the romance. Our lovers' talk evolves with our relationship and exists in things said and unsaid. The more you know, the more you can communicate. And the more you communicate, the stronger your relationship.

"I Love You"

Sometimes when we say, "I love you," we are saying that we love an image that we ascribe to. But real love exists on a full spectrum. It is just as powerful in the storms as it is in the sunshine. Don't let temporal disappointments or fluctuating circumstances rob you of the rewards of real love. Love is not fickle. It is forceful. It is a commitment of magnanimous proportions that stands firm where emotions wax and wane. There will definitely be times in your relationship when you are enraged, frustrated, disappointed, or distressed. There will also be times when you are exhilarated, enraptured, delighted, and smitten with ecstasy. This is perfectly normal. Emotions are meant to fluctuate and evolve. Otherwise, we wouldn't be human. But love does not react to emotion. Love is what grounds us. It is where the center of our relationship can exist.

Let go of your expectations of how love should express itself because everyone's interpretation is different. So many moms catch themselves thinking, *If my husband loved me, then he would . . .* But it just doesn't work that way. If, in your mind, love translates to certain actions and emotions, then you are just setting yourself up for disappointment. Love just is. And sometimes the unconditional loving is the hardest part. There is no valid interpretation for it, and you just have to know that it is there through all of the fickle emotions and scattered actions that characterize our lives.

TOTAL MOM TIP

Love Notes

When Blair and I were first married, we saved money by brown-bagging it to work and school every day. At first, I worked while he went to school. After a couple of years, he was the one working while I stayed home. First he made lunches for me, and then later I took over brown-bag duty. But always, there was a love note in the lunch sack. Now we both work out of the house, so we just leave love notes for each other on the bathroom mirror! Try this in your marriage. Slip little love notes in his lunch or leave a "ticket" on his windshield for him to find before he leaves for work. Sometimes we'll be sitting in the same room working on our laptops, and we'll send each other e-mail love notes. Get creative and think of ways to tell him he is loved.

"I Love Me"

You hardly ever hear about how important it is to love yourself in a relationship. It always seems to be about the other person. But I can tell you right now that what you bring to the table is just as important as what is sitting across from it. A person can only love you as much as you love yourself.

It's high time that moms began cultivating a little more self-love. We must be the most critical group of people in the world. How often do you smile at yourself in the mirror? Or announce your accomplishments to others? Don't dishonor yourself by criticizing who you are. So much potential and possibility lies within you, and so many attributes are already there. When you disparage your life, your dreams, your thoughts, your body, you do yourself a gross disservice. Don't shroud your brilliance! You are an amazing individual with a lot to offer, so let it shine.

If you really want to make a relationship work, then begin by appreciating yourself. How you feel about yourself will set the bar for how others feel about you. If you clothe yourself in criticism, then people will criticize you. If you think you are flawed, then people will see those flaws first before noticing anything else about you. If you feel that you deserve nothing, then that's exactly what you will get out of life — nothing. The energy you radiate will direct how a person relates to you. If you exude confidence and acceptance, then other people will absorb that emotion without even realizing it. You will be treated with respect, admiration, courtesy, and fondness when, and only when, you give others permission to do so. Your permission exists in the form of your self-esteem. Believe you are worthy of love, and love will be showered on you.

"I Like You"

You've got to love your husband — you vowed you would. But the liking part? Well, you didn't make any promises there. But maybe you should have. Relationships all begin with liking, and it is extremely important that this mutual fondness continues through all of the hills and valleys of a marriage. When you like a person, you enjoy sharing time with him and create opportunities to do so. Couples often get so caught up in establishing a healthy romance that they overlook a healthy friendship. Your husband needs to be your best friend. Intimacy is important, but real intimacy begins and ends with friendship.

Start looking for opportunities to celebrate your friendship and be together. You don't have to plan anything formal. As a matter of fact, the less pressure, the better. Whether you rock climb together or do yard work side by side, what is really important is that you seize every opportunity to share your life. When you keep talking and working together, you don't grow apart. Friendships fizzle and die out with a lack of attention. Stoke the fires of your relationship by remaining close friends.

> **TOTAL MOM TIP**
> **Step**
> **On Board the**
> **Friend Ship**
>
> Focus on your friendship by making time for totally sexless dates (of course, if some steamy lovemaking occurs, then I'm sure no one will complain). Date nights often fall into the routine of "sitter arrives; go out for dinner; sitter leaves; routine sex follows." Foster the friendship side by going sexless once in a while. Hire a sitter and go play laser tag, work out together, visit an art gallery, or take in a ball game. Be friends first and watch the relationship thrive.

A friend also recognizes the very best in you and inspires you to achieve it. Sometimes in a marriage, you want to see the best in your husband, so you tend to criticize him into being the best. That never works. Inspire him instead. Talk up his attributes, just like you would to a friend. Encourage him by being a mirror, reflecting back to him his very best self.

"I'm Proud of You"

Every single one of us, from infancy onward, thrives on feeling a sense of accomplishment and success. Try to look for ways to communicate pride to your husband on a daily basis, even if you really have to search for it ("You make that flannel shirt look really sexy!"). And when he experiences successes through his endeavors, let them be your successes as well. Flatter him and encourage him to accomplish even more. When it comes to nurturing, compliments go a lot further than criticism.

Showing your pride in another person doesn't just translate to showering him with compliments. Sometimes the best way to show pride in your husband is to fully accept and encourage his talents or interests. Sure, tinkering with his car in the garage every weekend or collecting Charlie Brown cartoons isn't netting you a single dime, but it is something he loves and it does not need to be validated. When you constantly ask why, you open the door to bitterness and frustration, two things that your marriage can definitely do without! It is pointless to ask why our husbands love certain things, why they can watch an entire day of football without moving off the couch, why they play video games with more enthusiasm than a ten-year-old boy, or why they still want to keep that neon Michelob sign from their frat house days. The point is, they love it, and that's enough reason to support them. My personal theory is that boys don't really grow up, they just change form and get a lot hairier. It's important to love your man, but also support and encourage that boy within.

Show your pride in his interests by sharing in them. Find out how his car engine works or learn some football plays so you can enjoy watching the game with him. I remember when Blair and I were first dating. He took me to a baseball game on one of our first dates. Of course, at the time, he had no idea that I had been the stats girl for the baseball team when I was in high school. The ball was knocked out to left field, popped off the fence, and snatched up by an outfielder. I remarked,

"That's a ground rule double!" He slowly turned his head and looked at me as if I were the *Sports Illustrated* swimsuit centerfold. I believe it was at that moment that he knew he had found his mate for life. The way to a man's heart is not through his stomach. It's through his interests and his accomplishments. Take pride in them.

Hopefully, most of your husband's interests are benign little hobbies that he holds on to. If, however, his little hobbies verge on the destructive, then you need to take a stand against them. Do not validate damaging habits—such as pornography, gambling, or any of the other habits that tear marriages apart—by blaming that boy within. Everyone has an inner sense of right and wrong. And anything that destroys is wrong, no question about it. Love him and love the marriage enough to stand up for what you know is right. But if his habits are safe, then by all means, encourage them.

"For You"

Real love is not a noun. It's a verb. Love becomes solid when your husband's happiness and fulfillment become yours as well. Logically, doing things for your husband should make you happy in return. I know sometimes it's not that easy, but try looking for opportunities to give instead of waiting to receive.

"For you" is doing things daily for your husband without any hidden agenda or anticipated reciprocity. Just do it because his fulfillment is your fulfillment. When you begin to look for opportunities to do for your husband, something amazing happens. He begins looking for opportunities to do for you. It's in the little things that love shows its face. It's making his cup of coffee before you make yours. It's rubbing his back when it's yours that is aching. A marriage is service with a smile, but it all comes back to you in huge rewards. Start fostering an attitude of giving with no strings attached. This is unconditional love at its best.

"I'm Sorry"

We are all guilty of doing stupid, selfish things. We all have a wicked witch within us that, given the right circumstances, will rear its ugly green head and set poor little scarecrows on fire. It's important to realize the depth of our ugliness so that we can redeem ourselves with the height of our beauty. But it all begins with learning to say, "I'm sorry."

Apologizing is an art form, and if your marriage is going to work, you've got to develop the art. First of all, see a problem for what it is. If trouble develops in your marriage and you truly look at yourself objectively, you may see something that's pretty darn ugly. Arguments are hardly ever one-sided, so hop in your husband's skin once in a while and try to see your actions and hear your words through his eyes and ears. You may be surprised when you see that green skin glowing underneath the pretty little pinafore of blamelessness. We are not as faultless as we would like to believe. It takes a lot of guts to step up to the plate and take some blame. But guts are a lot prettier than self-righteousness.

If you are at fault, don't waste time trying to explain, defend, or rationalize your words and actions. The only phrase that matters is "I'm sorry." Say it, get it over with, and then you can explain all you want later. Building bridges is often more difficult than tearing them down, but it's a lot easier to travel over a bridge than through a pile of rubble.

Focus on nurturing yourself through nurturing your marriage. It will all come back to you in waves of joy. This is your primary relationship. It will be the steam in your engine and the wind in your sails. And no amount of energy invested in your marriage is ever, ever wasted. Become fluent in lovers' talk and reap the rewards for the rest of your life.

Week Four, Day Five: Daily Exercises

1. In your journal, make a list of the things that first attracted you to your husband and the activities that you enjoyed together when you

were dating or first married. Sometimes when kids enter the picture, you lose track of what attracted the two of you to each other. Think back to those first flirty moments and write them down. Find some time within the next two weeks to do one of those activities together. This is a great way to foster the friendship side of your marriage.

2. Take some time today and write a love note to your husband. Be creative with this activity. For example, you could write a note that says, "You are more valuable to me than all the money in the world," and stick it in his wallet. Or maybe you could clean out his car for him and leave him a note on his steering wheel that says, "You drive me wild!"

3. Follow House Rule #4: Practice the Art of Camouflage. Pick up some pretty rugs for your home. Get a color that coordinates with your design while hiding dirt as much as possible, such as tan, brown, or a busy pattern.

Weekend Workout

Home: You're moving on to de-clutter Zone 3 this weekend. This may also be a good weekend to add some seasonal touches to your home. In the colder seasons, add some colorful throw blankets, deeper hues, scrumptious pillows, and maybe some dried flowers. In the warmer months, you may want to make it a bit more vibrant by adding some bright and cheerful hues, getting rid of heavy linens, and displaying some plants or colorful bouquets. Pick up some soy candles while you're at it to add some aroma to your home, perhaps fruits and florals in the warm months and some delicious dessert smells in the cold months. Practice House Rule #2: Clean When It's Dirty and House Rule #5: Set an Ultimatum by scheduling an event and inviting some friends over. You will be motivated to clean the house, but try not to go overboard. If it's not dirty, then don't clean it. Just get the house in good working order prior to the event.

Health: Continue to keep that B.A.D. C.R.A.P. out of your family's diet. And get in the kitchen and start cooking up some healthy family meals. Post your Pantry Planner on the fridge and start making your grocery list for next week's meals. If you use a magnetic gem clip to keep it posted, then you can slip any coupons into the clip and carry it all to the store in one envelope. This weekend, step up your workout a bit.

In addition to your morning walk, try doing an exercise video twice a week.

Family: Take time this weekend to attack that pile of photos you have stuck somewhere. File them away so that you can free yourself up to start creating and keeping some memories. Plan a fun family event, even if it's just making some nondairy sundaes this Sunday (get it? Sundaes on a Sunday?). You can even combine it with the above event (in the Home section of the Weekend Workout) and invite some friends over. Remember to take plenty of pictures, but don't just take shots of smiling faces. Document the action that is taking place—the baby eating with her hands, the dad with whipped cream on his nose, or the kids fighting over the chocolate syrup.

Life: Don't fall off the AM/PM routine wagon. Keep getting up early to have some special time just for you. If you need some incentive, then pick up a box of detox tea (Yogi Tea and Celestial Seasonings teas are some of my favorites) and a pretty new mug. Set it out on the counter before you go to bed so that you know it's waiting for you when you wake up in the morning. This is your time—enjoy it!

Congratulations!

You are nurtured inside and out, and it feels oh so good! Your home, health, family, marriage, and friends are all pouring energy and happiness into you as you pour it right back out. Now it's time to move on to Week Five!

CONFIDENT MOM

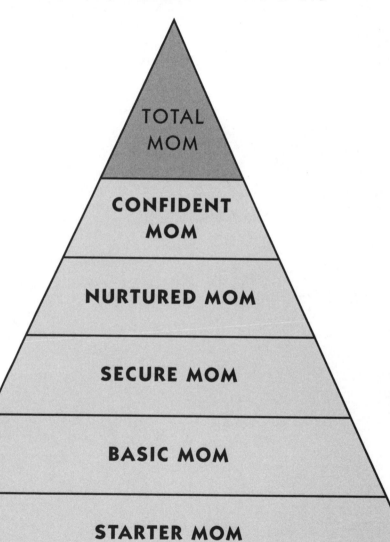

TOTAL MOM

CONFIDENT MOM

NURTURED MOM

SECURE MOM

BASIC MOM

STARTER MOM

Tuning Out, Tuning In

Most of us are guilty of going through intense phases of parental inadequacy. It usually happens just after we have collected enough parenting books to fill a bathtub and have every mom Web site bookmarked on our computers. We lie awake at night praying that we make it through motherhood alive and that we don't permanently damage our children in the process. But in an attempt to accumulate every bit of mothering knowledge available, we fill our brains with so much information that we crowd out our most valuable source of wisdom — our inner voice.

Be Selective

Gathering information is extremely important when it comes to raising our kids. We need to know when they should have their vaccinations, how to handle the tantrums, and how to help them when they reach the teen years. We want to collect everyone's opinions on parenting — the good, the bad, and the utterly ridiculous. It's perfectly normal to be "sponge mommies," absorbing everything around us and parenting by the book. But sooner or later you get to the point where you realize that in order to be a good parent you've got to be selective about the opinions, beliefs, and advice that you incorporate into your life. Parenting is a huge responsibility, so only let the best stuff make the cut.

But how do you determine what the best stuff is? Do you go by what your doctor tells you? Your mom? Your best friend? That expert with some initials after his name? Everyone parents differently, so how do you determine what advice to adhere to and what to throw out the window? In this regard, Socrates was right on the money when he said to "know thyself." The more you understand yourself, the better parent you will be.

When I first became a mother, I read every book I could find on parenting. In my mind, I had one shot at doing this thing, and I wanted to do it right. I had read that you should teach your child at an early age to go to sleep on her own and get accustomed to her crib as the place for sleeping. I tried to do this. I would put my daughter to bed and listen to her cry while I stood in the hallway, crying as well. I wanted to hold her, rock her, cuddle up in bed with her. But according to the experts, that wasn't the right thing to do. And, by golly, I was going to do this thing right!

Finally, out of complete exasperation with her crying herself to sleep and complete exhaustion from being up at night with her, I called my oldest sister. She listened to my sob story and simply said, "You already know what you want to do, so just go ahead and do it." That night, I nursed my baby, rocked her to sleep, laid her in her crib, and then brought her into bed with me to sleep when she woke in the night. We both slept so much better, and I have done the same with each child ever since. It may not work for some, but it certainly works for me and my family.

You already know what to do. You just may not be aware of it.

Take time to understand yourself. Listen to advice but hold it up to what your heart already believes and understands. If it doesn't sit well with your gut instinct, then throw it out. Some things are just objectively right or wrong. You always buckle up your child in a car seat. You never feed a baby honey. You definitely keep the knives out of reach.

These things are safety issues. But when the objective ventures into the subjective, the blacks and whites of parenting become various shades of gray. Things like sleep issues, discipline, and obedience fall into the unknown territory of parenting where you have to let your heart speak just as loudly as the experts. Listen to everyone and read everything, but always listen to your gut. If your gut says go, then go. If not, then keep searching for the techniques that work for you and your child.

Free at Last

Confidence is key when it comes to parenting. Kids are smart, and they can see through an act every time. There will always be times when we need to paint on a smile and stifle a scream, but living behind a facade is completely different. You should never subscribe to a belief system that does not acknowledge your identity. You are who you are, and you should embrace that completely. If every single mom is raising her children a certain way, that does not mean you should be. Question everything. If an opinion or a parenting technique fits with your character and what you want for your family, then adopt it as your own. But if not, then toss

TOTAL MOM TIP
Trust
Your Instincts

Moms are powerhouses when it comes to intuition. And the best way to become a more confident parent is to begin trusting in your intuition. That inner voice will freely guide you if you let it. Sometimes, even if there is no obvious reason why you are doing something, you need to do it—just because. Don't ever feel forced to defend your parenting style. I could argue all day that moms should share their beds with their babies, but that wouldn't do a bit of good, not for me and certainly not for someone who does not subscribe to that technique. Do what fits.

it out with last night's trash. Because if you try to live in a way that goes against your hardwiring, you will be fighting the natural flow of traffic. You will be uncomfortable with it. Your kids will be uncomfortable with it. And your attempts will eventually crash and burn. You were put on this earth to be the best person you can be, not the person who best fits in with the crowd around you.

Bigger Fish to Fry

I often see moms take on a lot of unnecessary anxiety. Motherhood is anxiety-provoking enough without us looking for more battles to fight. We must all do things that constantly push us out of our comfort zones. This is good and healthy. Motherhood is supposed to be uncomfortable now and then. If it wasn't, then you wouldn't be doing your job. However, you need to get to the point where you ask yourself if this anxiety is necessary or not. There are going to be awfully big fish to fry with your children, so choose your anxieties wisely. Feeling your insides knot up and your throat go dry is a perfectly natural part of motherhood. But when you feel those body cues, pause for a moment to question the logic behind your actions and decisions. Your gut may be telling you to lighten up.

Forcing a child to learn how to go to sleep on her own is unnecessary if you are more than willing to console her. Punishing her for coloring on the walls is unnecessary if you are willing to clean up after her. One day she will go to bed alone and one day she will quit coloring on the walls (either that or become an awesome graffiti artist). There are going to be enough stressful experiences you must go through as a mother, like allowing her to go out on a date or attend her first real party or go rock climbing. Fry the fish that are worth frying and throw the rest back into the lake. If you stress about everything, you're not going to have any lining left in your stomach by the time the kids go off to college.

Wisdom Works

You can educate yourself for years about parenting but still not have the wisdom to be a good parent. When God allowed Solomon to request anything he wanted, there was a good reason Solomon asked for wisdom over wealth, fame, or power. When you've got wisdom, you've got it all. If wealth, fame, and power come along later, then you are wise enough to appreciate them and use them effectively. If they don't, you are wise enough to enjoy life without them.

Wisdom is the key to effective parenting. Wisdom is what centers us. It is the *why* of mothering, while knowledge is the *how*. It is more important to know *why* your child wants to play sports than it is to know *how* he should play. It is more important to know *why* your child has a hard time concentrating than it is to know *how* to get him to remain on task. Wisdom should be first, but unfortunately, moms often have it backward. They want to know the how before they have first established the why. But knowledge can only go so far. Knowledge is finite. Wisdom, however, is infinite.

Every mom has access to wisdom, but very few actually take advantage of it. The reason for this is that wisdom is quiet yet powerful. And when all of the expert voices are silenced and common sense doesn't make sense anymore, we can free ourselves up to act on our intuition and allow wisdom to come into play. We can learn much from other moms who have been there and done that. They can advise on which pitfalls to avoid and how to find the hidden treasures along the way. But wisdom really shines when we listen to that inner voice and follow it, letting our own experiences and instincts direct us.

Read everything you can get your hands on; seek out advice from mothers who have gone through the fires that you feel are beginning to warm your toes; listen to your heart; question anything and everything. And when all is said and done, the list of pros and cons has been made, and logical plans have been laid out, just scrap it all and go with your gut.

Week Five, Day One: Daily Exercises

1. Think about some stressful parenting situations you have been facing lately. For example, potty training my first child was extremely stressful. I can actually remember crying over it. But looking back, I can see that my anxiety was not warranted. It yielded absolutely nothing productive and frustrated both of us. In your journal, write down these anxiety-producing situations you are experiencing as a mom.

2. Look at each one of these situations and take a moment to ask yourself if the anxiety is necessary and what it will yield that is productive. If it is not necessary, then come up with a coping technique that is more in tune with who you are and how you operate. For example, I modified my potty-training techniques greatly with subsequent children. I didn't rush the situation. Instead, I simply approached the issue once in a while and waited until each child was ready to initiate potty training. When they indicated they were ready, I took on the task. They were usually potty trained in less than a week, not because I did a great job teaching but because they were ready to learn. HUGE difference.

Power Moves

You can tell a confident mom a mile away. She has a certain way of walking and carrying herself that translates to "I know what I'm doing, so step aside." She is powerful and strong. Today you are going to wake up some of those muscles that have fallen asleep. You are going to stand tall and walk proud. Don't be surprised if people start moving out of your way!

Muscle Bound

Okay, so you're already walking. That's fantastic! You're watching what you eat as well. Way to go! So what's the point of working on your muscles? It's not like you are going to star in an action flick anytime soon. First, firm is a lot sexier than jiggly. When your body is toned and taut, then you don't have to worry about what is hanging over your bra strap or bulging out of your shorts. Second, muscle is a lot healthier than fat. When you have more muscle mass, you have more strength, more endurance, and more resistance to injury, and your body is able to function more efficiently. Third, muscle burns more calories than fat. That means that the higher percentage of muscle you have, the more calories you burn, even when you are just chilling in front of the TV.

Muscles develop through resistance. The more you use them, the firmer you become. In order to get into optimum shape, you need to combine cardio exercise (anything that gets your heart pumping) with strength training (anything that builds your muscles). Cardio melts off the fat, while strength training tones up what lies underneath. Most exercise programs, such as walking every morning, will accomplish both of these. When you are walking briskly you are increasing your heart rate. You are also working your muscles and strengthening your body, especially when you increase the intensity of the workout by using hand weights. But if you really want to see results quickly, then you should add strength training that targets specific parts of your body. And no matter what your schedule, budget, or current fitness level, there is definitely a way to incorporate strength training into your life.

Fitting It In

You don't have to live at the gym in order to tone your body. As a matter of fact, you can probably get better results at home because you can take advantage of the pockets of time that pop up during the day. I rarely have a lengthy amount of time that I can dedicate to exercise (other than the thirty minutes I grab every morning to go walking while the kids are still asleep). Any strength training or additional exercise has to be squeezed in to my already crowded schedule. Here are the best ways I have found to work my body while I am working on the home, family, and everything else in my life.

1. **Include the kids.** They learn early that if they can't beat you, they might as well join you. It is extremely difficult to keep the kids occupied while you try to exercise, so why not do both at the same time? Children of all ages love to work out. Older kids can follow fitness videos along with you. If they don't want to follow along, then they can at least sit on your feet while you do sit-ups. If you have older tweens or teens, then find some videos that have hip-hop

BUDGET GYM MUST-HAVES

You can carve out a home gym on any budget. All you need is a corner of your home and some of these essentials:

Hand weights: These are perfect for resistance training for your arms and back, as well as your abs, butt, and thighs when you do crunches or squats. Don't get adjustable ones because they are too clumsy and time consuming. Just get a variety of individually weighted dumbbells.

Ankle weights: These are not a necessity, but they are great to use when you are doing leg lifts or cycling. They really help tone your abs, hips, and legs. Avoid heavy leg weights when you walk because they can cause muscle strain.

Exercise mat: The floor can become particularly hard and unforgiving on the fourth rep of crunches. A mat helps ease the discomfort and can be wiped clean after you work up a sweat.

Resistance bands: These are perfect for doing resistance training on your legs and arms. You can also use them to work your back, which all moms need a little help with.

Exercise ball: This wonderful multipurpose tool helps strengthen your core. An added benefit is that the kids love to play with it!

Step: No butt should be without one. Get a step that has folding legs so that you can just slide it under a sofa or bed. Using a step really helps tone your lower body, especially your butt and thighs.

Instructional videos: None of this equipment will do you any good if you don't know how to use it. Make sure you get some videos that have received good reviews from real women, and get a variety so that you won't get bored. In my collection, I have some fun and easy dance videos so the kids can enjoy exercising with me, as well as some more intense strength-training videos that I use once in a while.

moves and watch them jump up and join in. Younger children love to do easier dance fitness videos, such as Richard Simmons. You can always increase the intensity of the workout by using free weights. Even the littlest ones can work out with you by becoming the cutest weights you've ever seen. I have put my little ones on my abs while I did butt lifts or let them ride on my back while I did leg lifts. They have fun, my muscles get a workout, and everyone's happy.

2. **Add some moves to your daily routine.** Little steps here and there can make a world of difference. Doing forty leg lifts may seem like a big deal, but doing five on each side every time you wash dishes is nothing. If you add little moves here and there, you'll be surprised at the amount of toning you can sneak in during the day. When you bend down to pick up toys, tone up your butt and thighs by going into a full squat. When you play with your baby, you can tone your shoulders and arms by lifting her up laterally in front of you. And if you really feel up to it, you can bring out Twister for family game night.

3. **Make it a habit.** If strength training becomes a regular part of your day or week, then you will definitely see results. When I return from my morning walk, I immediately lie on my back in the living room, put my weights on my chest, and do some crunches. I follow that with some butt lifts. Then I stand up, do some leg lifts, and get on with my day. It's not much, but those little steps help me stay in shape because I have made them a habit.

Work That Body

Your body changes dramatically after you have a baby, but you can still whip it in to shape. Here are the areas of the body that most moms need to target:

Back: Pregnancy, childbirth, and the inevitable child lugging that follows do a hack job on our backs. When your back is strong, all your other physical responsibilities—from carrying groceries to planting annuals—are easier. Unfortunately, this critical part of your body is often neglected. The most important step you can take to strengthen your back is to maintain good posture. Become conscious of how you carry yourself. Make a habit of pausing for a few seconds during the day—perhaps when your hourly alarm goes off—to check your posture. Roll your shoulders back and stand up straight, as if there is a string attached to your spinal cord and coming through the top of your head, holding you up.

> **TOTAL MOM TIP**
> **Back**
> **in Shape**

A great way to develop your back muscles is to lie on your bed on your stomach, bent over the side with your chest hanging off the bed. Cross your arms in front of your chest, lift up your torso, and then slowly drop back down. Do as many reps as you can without straining yourself. Don't do these immediately after you wake up because your back has not had a chance to warm up. A good time to do these is when you are going to bed at night.

Abdomen: Be patient with your abs. They have done a lot for you. As you practice good posture, also be conscious of tightening up your abs by holding in your stomach. Crunches also strengthen and tone your abs. And little kids love sitting on your feet while you do sit-ups!

Legs: The key to keeping your legs toned is to keep them moving. When you go to the park, don't be one of the benchwarmers. Get up and climb, run, slide, and stretch. When you need something, don't send one of the kids after it; get up and get it yourself. The more you use your legs, the better shape they will be in. Another good way to tone is to strap on some ankle weights while you are working in the kitchen and do some leg lifts to the back and side.

Butt: Slow, deep squats are a great way to tone this area. You can further concentrate your efforts by holding free weights on your shoulders. But, as always, moms have to be creative. Why not do some squats when you are carrying your child in a backpack? The kids love it. Your butt and thighs hate it (but will thank you later)!

Arms: Most moms are guilty of the single-arm strategy, where we use only one arm to carry our kids, groceries, and that huge handbag. As a result, our arms look like Popeye on one side and Olive Oyl on the other. Strengthen both arms by taking turns carrying the weight and shifting it back and forth. And when you pick up things around the house, don't swing your arms and use momentum to lift them. Instead, lift items slowly and feel your arm muscles working.

Begin focusing your efforts on strength training and watch it pay off. You'll look stronger and feel stronger. And before you know it, your kids will have a hard time keeping up with YOU!

Week Five, Day Two: Daily Exercises

1. In your journal, write down at least three effective ways to incorporate strength training into your daily routine. For example, you may have stairs that you can climb ten times every day or some strength-training videos that you can use two to three times a week.

2. Take action on one of these strength-training exercises today. But remember to make it into a habit by doing it regularly. Decide during your PM routine what exercise activity you are going to do the next day and plan your outfit accordingly. Are you doing an exercise video? Lay out your cross-trainers and some workout clothes. Are you spending twenty minutes in the morning doing yoga? Lay out nonbinding clothes and yoga shoes. Are you planning on taking the kids to the park? Put out some comfy sneakers and blue jeans.

Your Happy Place

You were designed for something remarkable. No one can fulfill this purpose like you can. Motherhood can be your greatest achievement, but it does not necessarily have to be your only achievement. It's easy to get so immersed in your career as a mom that you lose a sense of the woman inside. Don't let this happen. You are the engine of your family. Because of this responsibility, you need to take the time necessary to fill up your tank. This week is a perfect time to focus on your personal skills and passions—to discover them, shine them up a little, or even turn them into a rewarding hobby or thriving side business.

You have unique abilities that bring you true fulfillment, but only when they are put into practice. Perhaps you love to play the piano. You may be an excellent gardener, or maybe you can cook up a storm in the kitchen. Whatever it is, there is something that gives you splendid joy. This is the thing you were meant to do. Raising my children gives me ultimate joy, but I also receive personal gratification from writing, speaking, and entertaining. If I denied myself this gratification, I would eventually shrivel up, with all of the creative juices drained out of me. You need to fill yourself up so that you can pour yourself out. Whatever it is that brings you personal happiness, you need to act on it. This is your happy place, and it's a great place to live. Look within yourself to

197

find this place. So often, we look for greatness outside of ourselves. We see our neighbors' achievements and decide that we should strive for the same thing. Then we are stumped when it doesn't work out for us. Discover your own personal genius. Mine for the gems in your own field. You have treasures waiting to be discovered.

Discovering Your Place

"What would you do if you knew you could not fail?"
— ROBERT H. SCHULLER

What are you passionate about? What could you talk about for hours or attend a conference on? My husband's father is obsessed with ancient artifacts. Some of his best stories are from the days when he attended archaeological digs or went on camping trips in the desert, searching for fossilized coins or bones. He could talk about the subject for hours. He is happiest in his wide-brimmed hat and boots, reaching through time, space, and sand to touch a civilization long gone. That is his happy place, his idea of heaven. For me, camping in the desert and eating canned rations seems more like a trip to hell.

What is your happy place? When do you feel most complete and alive? I believe that many of us spend so much time in the place we feel we *should* be that we neglect the place we *could* be. My brother is happiest and most complete when he is cooking extravagant dishes. Watching him in the kitchen is like watching a well-choreographed dance. He pours his passion into his meals. But he works as a financial consultant because he feels that is what he *should* be doing. That is what supports the family. I respect his sense of obligation. It would be foolish to drop everything and take a new career path. But everyone could benefit from a bit of foolishness now and then.

As you set out to discover your happy place, think back on what brought you joy as a child as well as what brings you joy today. I should have known early on that I was destined for motherhood. My favorite activities when I was a child were spending time in the woods preparing food (usually moss pâté on bark chips or mushroom-and-grass soup) for my baby dolls and dressing up my fat cat, Max, in a gown and bonnet and feeding him a baby bottle full of milk. I also loved to draw, write, and make up stories. At the age of nine I published a community newsletter titled the *PMA Times* (*PMA* stood for Positive Mental Attitude). I even went around the neighborhood and solicited subscriptions! As a grown-up, I am still doing the same things I enjoyed as a child. I am raising my beautiful babies (kind of like my fat cat, Max, minus the claws and the fur) as well as writing, speaking, and building my own business.

> **TOTAL MOM TIP**
> **Let's Go to the Library**
>
> Start mining for those gems within you. The next time you take the kids to the library, take some time for yourself. Peruse the nonfiction aisles and see if anything strikes your fancy. Thumb through pages. If anything jumps out at you, then try your hand at it. I have a friend who loves to sew. She stumbled across a small book of handbag designs and decided to try creating a few of her own. She sewed up some samples for her own use. A store owner happened to see one of them slung over her shoulder and offered to sell them for her. She now sells her handbags in boutiques all across Florida and is considering expanding nationally. You never know what can happen, so don't limit the library visits to preschool story time. Take some time for yourself as well.

Turn Your Passion into Product

I've always heard that you should work like you don't need the money. Those words didn't console me too much when we were worried about scraping together enough money to buy bread and peanut butter for sandwiches, but it is so true. You only have one shot at life. Why spend it doing something unfulfilling? Yes, you do need money. But all the money in the world won't satisfy you if you're living outside of your true calling. Let your work be your joy, and your joy be your work.

As a mom, you may or may not carry the responsibility of contributing financially to the family. If you don't, then that frees you up a bit more to invest your time and energy into something you enjoy. But the obligation to earn money should never be a reason not to pursue your dreams. On the contrary, it should propel you to go further and higher, to struggle even more because you are powered by passion. When you really and truly love what you do, the money will come. I know those words sound a bit trite and shallow, but they're true. Even during those times Blair and I would lie awake at night wondering why we ever started our own business and how we were going to pay the bills, we would wake up the next morning ready to give it another shot and push through the next barrier. The reason? We love what we do. The world will bend to your wishes when you are persistently living in line with your distinct calling. The money will come. It may not come on *your* time, but it will come when the time is right.

If you would like to earn money by pursuing your dreams, then consider turning your passion into product. If you love to make soap, then package some bars and sell them at a craft fair. If you love to sing, then grab your guitar and perform at a local coffeehouse. You never know where one small action can take you. And you never *will* know — until you try. All real successes begin with one small act of passion.

The Upside of Failure

Many times, people refrain from pursuing their dreams or turning their passion into product because they are afraid of failing. But the good news is that failure is inevitable. I know it doesn't sound like good news, but once you fully acknowledge that you are going to trip and fall, you are free to run with abandon.

Listen to the spirit within you. This is the voice that can lead you. This is the spirit that knows where all of those gems are hidden within you. Your mind has the pickax, but your soul has the map. Let her guide you. If you can't recall what brings you deep joy today, take the time to search for it. Mine for it night and day if you have to. And when you find your joy, your happy place, offer it up to a world that has been patiently waiting for you to arrive.

Week Five, Day Three: Daily Exercises

1. Grab that journal and start mining for gems! Think of the personal activities you enjoy doing for hours on end, those activities that leave you filled instead of drained, energized instead of exhausted. It could be anything—cooking, writing, studying herbal medicine, anything. If you're having a hard time coming up with activities, think back to when you were a child. What were the things that brought you fulfillment? Take a moment and write them down.

2. Look over those activities. Are you allotting enough time in your schedule to enjoy them? If not, maybe you can set aside some time on a weekly basis or during your AM routine. If you are currently enriching your life with these activities, then consider turning the hobby into a profession. Can you take those watercolors you painted and turn them into greeting cards to sell at the craft fair? Can you take those poems you wrote and submit them for publication? Think of some ways you can capitalize on your talents and write them down. You can even use Action Skill #2: Take Baby Steps and plot out daily or weekly tasks that will help you reach a larger goal. Don't forget to schedule these on your calendar and follow through.

You Glow, Girl!

"Zest is the secret of all beauty. There is no beauty that is attractive without zest."

— CHRISTIAN DIOR

I t's true. When you look good you feel good. I can preach inner beauty all day long, but there's no getting around the fact that our appearance really and truly matters—a lot! You can be drop-dead gorgeous on the inside, but if you look like you don't give a hoot about the outside, then that's all people are going to see. This week of building confidence is a perfect time to spruce up your appearance, because your looks dramatically affect your attitudes. Beauty is not this strange, elusive trait that you either have or don't have. Beauty is a characteristic that we should nurture every day, on both the inside and the outside. If you are a loving mother, then there's no doubt that you have that inner beauty part taken care of. Now take some time to let that beauty adorn the outside as well.

Skin Deep

Your skin is the largest organ that you have, and it operates like a readout of your health. When you're healthy, it glows. When you are not healthy, it is dull and washed out. You've probably already noticed an improvement in your skin as a result of the improvement in your diet. You can make your skin even more radiant by treating it with quality care. Follow these steps for glowing skin:

◎ **Keep it clean.** Dirt and bacteria can clog your pores and result in a dull complexion and even adult acne. Wash your face every morning and evening with a nondrying cleanser. Remember, as you get older, your beauty products need to be modified. Stripping cleansers may have been perfect for your late teens, when you were pumping out facial oil by the gallon. But as you age, you produce less and less oil, so your cleansers need to be milder and more moisturizing.

◎ **Exfoliate regularly.** Your skin is constantly renewing its cells. However, as you get older, this regeneration process slows down. You can help it along by exfoliating regularly. When you help your skin shed old cells, you assist with the renewal process. You don't need any expensive kits or an in-house dermatologist. All you need is an abrasive pad designed for faces. Use this at least once every other day with your cleanser to help shed old skin cells and freshen your appearance.

TOTAL MOM TIP
Smooth Move

Foundation does a great job of smoothing out your complexion. But if you're not the makeup type, consider trying out a tinted moisturizer. That way, you get all the benefits of a face lotion as well as the smoothing properties of a foundation.

◎ **Moisturize.** I thought I would never need a facial moisturizer. I always had the shiniest face in the crowd. But a good quality lotion does three things. It moisturizes your skin, slows the aging process by treating skin with beneficial ingredients, and protects your skin by acting as a barrier against harmful elements, such as pollution and, if it contains SPF, sunlight. Don't skip the lotion, even if your skin shows no signs of dryness. There are plenty of good lotions developed for your skin type, even if it's oily. And quality lotions don't have to cost an arm and a leg. There are lots of great choices at your local drugstore.

Hair, There, and Everywhere

Scream it out from the mountaintops: "NO MORE MOM HAIR!" I'll never forget the day my ten-year-old daughter came to me and asked, "Is there a certain age when a woman has to get her hair all cut off and make it curly?" Don't fall into the mom-hair trap. And if you are already there, then here's how to dig yourself out.

◉ **Keep it current.** Don't let your hairstyle get dated. If you've had the same hairstyle for the last six years, then chances are you need some emergency intervention. Next time you are at the grocery store, pick up a copy of a hairstyle magazine and circle any styles that you like.

YOUR KITCHEN SPA

You have a perfect spa right in your kitchen! Here are some quick and easy ways to get salon beauty in your own home at a fraction of the cost.

Hair mask: You should occasionally give your hair a deep-conditioning treatment. For dry hair, grab some mayonnaise (the full-fat kind, not light or fat-free) and work it through your hair, starting at the scalp and massaging it down to the ends. Now stick it all under a shower cap and let it penetrate for at least thirty minutes. You can help it along by heating it with a hair dryer. Then wash hair.

Product remover: Hair can become weighted down with products after a while. To rejuvenate it, just put some apple cider vinegar in a spray bottle, saturate your hair, let it sit for a few minutes, and then rinse it out with cool water.

Favorite facial mask: Mix up one egg white, a few drops of olive oil, and a bit of yogurt. Apply it to your face, chill in front of the television

Take that magazine to the best salon you can afford and talk to one of the stylists to see what will and will not work with your hair and face. Many moms have only one request—they want something easy. Easy doesn't always translate to attractive. It's worth spending a few minutes on your hair in the morning to make you look good and feel good.

- **Accessorize.** Consider your hair a fashion accessory. Have fun with it. Take some time to check out all of the cool hair accessories that are in department stores now. No matter what your length, style, or texture, there are some awesome doodads to wear in your hair. Perhaps you can style it up in a twist with some jeweled pins or maybe just slap on a braided leather headband. Whatever you do, it's your hair, so enjoy it.

- **Care for it.** If you neglect your hair, then your hair will look, well,

for about fifteen minutes, and then rinse it off at a commercial break.

Facial scrub: Cornmeal makes an excellent exfoliating scrub. Just put a spoonful in your hand, mix it up with some cleanser or even some olive oil, scrub your face with it, and follow with a cool rinse.

Anti-aging treatment: This treatment works as a mild acid peel. Get a slice of fresh pineapple or papaya and smear it all over your face, avoiding your eyes. Let it sit for about five minutes or until you feel your skin beginning to tingle. Rub a spoonful of baking soda onto your skin to neutralize the acid and exfoliate the tissue, and then follow with a rinse.

Eye makeup remover: Keep a small bottle of olive oil in the bathroom cabinet to take off your eye makeup at night.

Facial toner: Apple cider vinegar comes to the rescue again.

Lip plumper: One of the main ingredients in many lip plumpers is cayenne pepper. Just rub your lips with some Tabasco sauce (if you can stand it—remember, it's hot stuff!).

neglected. Your hair gets exposed to pollution, sunlight, chlorine, and other things that can strip it of shine and luster. Take a few minutes at least once a month (once a week is even better) to put a deep-conditioning mask on your hair. And if you have highlights or color in your hair, then consider using a color-specific shampoo to brighten up the hue a bit. And don't forget to make regular trips to your salon to keep those ends trimmed and your mane looking healthy.

Tough as Nails

My daughters and I visit a retirement home every other week to give the elderly women manicures. You can always tell so much about the women by their nails. All of them are very old, but the ones who have healthy diets and get regular exercise have healthy, strong nails. The ones who are munching on cupcakes and candy have brittle, yellowed, or weak nails. If you want to have healthy nails, then make sure you have a healthy diet and lifestyle. Aside from that, here are some more tips for your tips.

- **Give them a break.** Let your nails take an occasional break from polish, or else they can become yellowed. When you do go without polish, give yourself a cuticle treatment by massaging some olive oil into your nails and nail beds.

- **Keep the cuticle.** Cuticles protect your nail beds, so resist the urge to trim them. If hangnails are a problem, then keep those trimmed. But all you should need to do to your cuticles is push them back occasionally with an orange stick. You should do this after you have taken a hot shower or washed some dishes so that the tissue is softened.

- **Buff them up.** Buffing nails is an excellent choice for moms because we want pretty nails, but polish constantly chips off. Buffing your nails makes it look as if you have clear polish on because it shines up your nails into a gleaming finish. A four-sided buffer is even better because it files, smoothes, buffs, and shines—an entire manicure in one tool.

Your smile speaks volumes about you. But the question is, what is it saying? Go ahead and flash those pearly whites in the mirror and see if they are really as pearly white as they should be. Your first priority should be getting dental checkups twice a year. If you want to brighten your smile a bit more, then pick up some teeth-whitening strips. Use them while you take a shower and get dressed in the morning. Just don't forget like I did, and leave them in when you go grocery shopping. If you do, it's a guarantee that you will run into at least three people you know!

TOTAL MOM TIP
Smile Awhile

A Touch of Color

Ever since the first day that I gazed into the pages of *Teen* magazine, I was enamored with makeup. I still remember that tiny box with a bottle of beige CoverGirl makeup and a powder compact that my mom gave me for my thirteenth birthday. It was her signal that I was finally allowed to wear makeup, and it was as if the gates of heaven opened and I heard a chorus of angels singing. I still love makeup—not because of how it covers up but because of how it accentuates.

- ◉ **Take Time:** You always have time to put on a little bit of makeup, even if it's just a dab of lip gloss at a traffic light or a few strokes of blush to bring out your natural glow. A few minutes spent accentuating your natural beauty will give you the boost of confidence that you need to carry you throughout your day.
- ◉ **Fresh and Fabulous:** Keep your makeup routine fresh. Colors change with seasons, and new products come out every month. Try out a few. Find out from your friends what their favorite products are or read customer reviews on www.Beauty.com.

◎ **Read Up:** Beauty magazines, such as *Allure* or *Glamour,* are great resources to find out what's hot and what's not. They can also help keep you current on makeup trends. Get a subscription and keep a current copy in your bathroom or by your bed, places where you are more likely to have five minutes to yourself to flip through some pages.

◎ **Frame of Mind:** Keep in mind that all of the concealer and every shade of eye shadow under the sun won't do you a bit of good unless you have the right frame of mind. You are beautiful just as you are. Makeup only helps you put your best face forward.

Week Five, Day Four: Daily Exercises

1. Think back to your first experiences with the concept of beauty. Did you grow up feeling beautiful and confident? Was makeup used to conceal flaws or to accentuate natural beauty? What were the messages that you received about beauty or cosmetics? Take a few moments to write down your thoughts in this area. After you do this, think about all of the reasons that you deserve to feel beautiful and pampered. Write down one statement that affirms your freedom to put beauty into practice, such as "I deserve to be attractive, and I will take time every day to feel beautiful, look beautiful, and pamper my beautiful body."

2. In your journal, write down at least three things you can add to your beauty routine. It may be a weekly pedicure or a new hairstyle, but think of a few things that can make you look good and feel good. And don't use the excuse that you have no time. My entire makeup routine in the morning takes about five minutes. There's always time to sneak in some beauty. Now do it!

Let There Be Organization

As you de-clutter the different zones in your house, you need to devise a plan to keep them that way. You can accomplish this through proper organization. An organized home makes you feel confident and in control. Now I'm not saying you need to alphabetize your sock collection. An organized home does not have to be pristine and perfect (unless you are pristine and perfect — but then, why would you be reading this book?). In order for organization to work for the long haul, you have to organize your home around who you are and how you work. And everyone is different, so every organizational system will be different. As a matter of fact, the only criteria for successful organization is that you know where everything is and can get to it quickly and efficiently. If you have already accomplished that, then kudos to you! But if not, or if your organizational skills need a bit of tweaking, then read on.

Pop the Three Big Questions

It doesn't take a weekend retreat, online classes, or months of therapy to be organized. And contrary to popular belief, being organized is not a genetic trait that you may or may not inherit. Anyone and everyone can be organized. But all great organization begins with three big questions.

If you can answer them, then you can create and maintain an organized home. They are:

1. What activity goes on here?
2. What supplies are needed for this activity?
3. What container can hold these supplies?

Don't run out and grab some bins and baskets to organize stuff. The first thing you need to use when organizing your home is your head. Think through everything so that you can do it right the first time and not waste time and energy creating a system that doesn't work for you. Abraham Lincoln once said that if he had eight hours to chop down a tree, he would spend six hours sharpening his ax. Well, consider these three questions a way to sharpen your ax for some serious organization.

Question #1: What *Activity* Goes On Here?

If you manage a busy family, you already know that many activities go on in your home. And if you are striving for organization, there should be a designated spot for each one. The important thing, however, is not to create a space for each activity but to analyze where the activity is already taking place. When you organize around how you are already living, then you don't have to bother teaching yourself and your family new routines. You simply apply structure to your current patterns. It couldn't be easier. For example, I read magazines in bed, so that is the spot where all the magazines go when they come into the house, in a metal basket right beside the bed. The kids take off their shoes after they walk through the front door, so that is the spot where all of the shoes go, in a big washtub in the foyer. We pay bills in the home office, so when mail comes in, the bills are immediately tossed into a drawer in the office.

When you begin organizing your home, don't try to do it all in one fell swoop. If you do, you'll be up to your ears in mass confusion. Simply do one zone at a time. Take a moment to look at it logically. Ask yourself what activity is taking place in this zone and use that as your starting point to apply some form of organization. For example, if your current de-cluttering zone is your living room, ask yourself what activities take place there. Is it watching television? Entertaining guests? Playing games? Reading? Don't try to figure out what activities *could* take place in the zone. Ask yourself what activities are *already* taking place in the zone.

Be Logical

When you begin analyzing the activities that go on in your home, make sure you apply some logic to the situation. Don't fight the natural flow of traffic in your home. Work with it instead. You may love the idea of a home office stuck in a back room upstairs. But if all of the bills get thrown into a nook in the kitchen, then maybe that needs to be the spot where you create a home office. Go ahead and turn the room upstairs into a guest retreat.

I was in "zone denial" for quite a long time when it came to home-schooling my kids. We always started in the schoolroom that I had set up in the basement. However, by lunchtime the kids began wandering upstairs to be closer to the kitchen (the hub of all family activity). Finally, after I noticed that books, folders, and workbooks were stacking up along the wall in the dining room, I realized that I had to make a change. I turned the room in the basement into a playroom and installed some shelves in the dining room to hold all of the school stuff. I was able to organize logically around the way we were living instead of trying to structure our lives around the organization.

Include Everything

When you are planning for organization, make sure you take the time to consider every activity that goes on in your zone. You may not like that the kids throw their backpacks and lunch boxes on the kitchen counter every time they walk in the back door, but the fact of the matter is that they do. It's the closest and most convenient place for them to set down their stuff. Instead of chewing them out for it, just organize around it. Perhaps you could install some hooks underneath the counter or place a wicker laundry basket beside the back door to hold their stuff.

As you continue de-cluttering your zones, add organization to the process. After you toss out all of the throwaways and giveaways, take what is left and put it through the three-question organizing process. This finishing step will enable you to keep the zones clutter-free. Afterward, when you cycle back through zones, all you have to do is some deep cleaning and make sure that everything remains organized and clutter-free.

Question #2:
What *Supplies* Are Needed for This Activity?

Once you decide what activities take place in each zone, you can figure out what supplies are needed. For example, if you are organizing the garage and one of the activities in that zone is to house sports equipment, then the next step is to decide what supplies are needed for that activity. For my family, it would be roller skates, hockey sticks, soccer balls, bats, gloves, baseballs, basketballs, a badminton set, tennis rackets and balls, bikes, scooters, skateboards, helmets, and pads. It's important that you list every single item so that you can devise an organized way to store it all.

Don't forget about the little details. For example, for reading magazines, I need to make sure that there is adequate reading light. These details need to be listed under the supplies as well. If the kids like to play games in the living room, they don't just need games, they also need a flat surface to play on as well as some floor cushions that they can scatter around for seating. This is part of good organization, planning around the natural living process and remembering all the details that are part of it.

Question #3:
What *Container* Can Hold These Supplies?

This is where you pull it all together in a way that works for you. After you come up with all of the supplies that are needed for the activity, sort them into categories, figure out the size and type of container you need, and *then* go get the containers. Do not go buy a bunch of containers before you go through this three-question process, or else you run the risk of getting the wrong size, too many, or too few. Do it right the first time.

Finding the right size containers is key. If a container is too small, then stuff goes spilling out everywhere. If it's too big, then it can become a catchall and hold clutter that doesn't necessarily belong to the activity at hand. This applies to even the smallest of things. For example, I have a basket on my kitchen counter that holds fruit. If our fruit supply gets low, then kids start sticking junk in the basket when they help pick up around the house. The other day, all we had in the basket was one tiny apple, two bananas, a pair of socks, and a Lego knight! Make sure you size your containers correctly!

TOTAL MOM TIP
Show Some Style

No matter what your design tastes are, there are appealing ways to contain your belongings, so don't think for a minute that you are relegated to cast-off shoe boxes and old laundry baskets. After you sort through your supplies, get something that not only holds your belongings but looks good doing it. Kids play with toys in the living room, but you wouldn't know this at first glance because all of their toys are organized into cute open baskets that are displayed on a set of bookshelves. Get containers that work but, more important, get containers that work for you and your specific style. Perhaps you could use a small flowerpot to store your car keys or an antique wooden bin to hold your makeup.

Sort It All

Before you buy any containers, organize your supplies into categories. For example, with the sports gear I mentioned earlier, I sorted the supplies into long stuff (bats, hockey sticks), round stuff (balls, pucks), riding stuff (bikes, scooters), wearable stuff (skates, helmets), little stuff (birdies, golf and tennis balls, grip tape for skateboarding, gloves, pads), and stuff that I could hang up (skateboards, rackets). This way, I could look at everything and see what I needed to get in order to contain it. For the long stuff and the tall stuff, I got two large trash cans, one for sticks and bats, the other for balls. For the riding stuff, I got a bike rack that rests on the ground so that the kids could be responsible for putting away their own bikes and scooters. For the wearable stuff, I got a large plastic tote for skates, and I have the kids strap their helmets on their bike seats when they're not in use. For the little stuff, I got a plastic container with clearly labeled drawers to divide up the contents, and for hanging stuff, I got large hooks and put them on the wall. There! It's like a beautiful puzzle that all comes together in an orderly fashion, and it makes my life easier and more manageable.

Organization can do that for you. One day, your home seems to be a chaotic mess. But if you just take a moment to clear out the clutter and structure it around how you live your life, then you find that you have more time, more productive energy, and a peace of mind that you had not experienced before.

Week Five, Day Five: Daily Exercises

1. Being organized can help your home, family, and life run so much smoother. What are the reasons for you to be organized? For example, perhaps you need to spend less time searching for lost items. Maybe your home gets messy because there is not a designated spot for the kids to store their toys and other belongings. Or perhaps

you realize that you could get a lot more accomplished during the day if you were better organized. Take a moment and write down at least five of these reasons.

2. Your next de-cluttering spot is Zone 4. Write "Zone 4" at the top of a new page in your journal. Then draw two lines down the middle of the page, dividing it into three columns. Mark these columns Activities, Supplies, and Containers. Under the Activities column, write down all of the activities that occur in Zone 4, leaving plenty of space between them. Under the Supplies column, write down all of the supplies that you need for those activities, remembering to include the details. Now under the Containers column, write down the containers you need to store those supplies. Try to save some money by using what you already have. If you need to pick up some storage containers, list them on your Pantry Planner under Miscellaneous. The next time you go to the grocery store, you can consolidate your errands and pick up the containers, too.

WEEK FIVE

Weekend Workout

Home: This weekend you are beginning de-cluttering Zone 4 of your home. You already did the groundwork on Day Five by establishing the activities, supplies, and containers that you need for that zone. Now when you de-clutter, you can sort the supplies and store them in appropriate containers before you put them away. Remember, the little steps are the ones that will get you where you want to be. If you do one zone at a time, your entire home will soon be de-cluttered, organized, and running smoothly. After you complete the zone, reward yourself with something special for that space in your home—maybe some pretty new hangers for your closet or matching baskets for the toy room. It doesn't need to cost a lot, and the little expenditure will pay off in a huge way when your home is neat, pared down, and running beautifully.

Health: Are you staying away from the B.A.D. C.R.A.P.? Remember to keep fueling your body for optimum performance. And keep increasing the F.I.T. levels of your workout. By now, you should be able to make your workouts more frequent, more intense, or longer. If you don't already have some, get ankle weights and wear them this weekend whenever you do work in the kitchen. This way, you can incorporate strength training by doing leg lifts while you are washing dishes or preparing meals. If your morning exercise is walking, then add some lightweight hand weights to your workout and extend your walk by 25 percent (if you are walking one mile, extend it to 1¼ miles).

Family: Think of a great outing that the family can go on this weekend. Remember, family events don't always require tons of planning. Feel free to gather up the kids and a picnic basket and go do something, even if it's just reading a book together at the park. Try not to be so constrained by what you *should* be doing and follow your gut a bit more when it comes to raising your kids. Here are some ideas to get you thinking outside the box:

- Have a picnic on a blanket, even if there are plenty of tables at the park.
- Visit the planetarium and lie on the floor to gaze at the stars instead of sitting.
- Go on a late-night date with your child and talk together, *really* talk.
- Take a trip to the toy store, just to play with the toys, not to buy any.
- Visit a skate park and let your child teach you some moves.
- Take your child on a walk and stand in the path of every sprinkler you see.

Life: Being confident also means being competent. Take that one thing, that passion that you have, and channel your energy into strengthening your skills in this area. You may even find that your talents could earn some money. Write up a mini business plan that lists what you would need to turn your skills into a business, who would buy what you have to sell, and how and where you would sell it. Get some advice and opinions from objective friends. And take some chill time for yourself this weekend and flip through some fashion and beauty magazines for some pampering tips.

Congratulations!

Can you believe you only have one more week to go? I am so excited for you! You are confident and glowing, all because you decided that you deserved more and took action to get it. Now it's time to move on to the final week — Week Six!

Week Six

TOTAL MOM

CONFIDENT
MOM

NURTURED MOM

SECURE MOM

BASIC MOM

STARTER MOM

Perception Is Everything

For some reason, once a woman becomes a mother, her inner critic goes into overdrive. You are emerging as a Total Mom, and you need to embrace every aspect of who you are—the positive, the negative, and everything in between. It's important always to strive for improvement—not because you are unhappy about who you are, but because you know you deserve the best. Self-love motivates you by pulling you forward. Self-loathing just holds you back. Moms are notorious for hating how they look, how they think, how they feel, and even how they parent. You have come this far, and you know by now that positive attracts positive. If you want to be your best, then you need to love everything that makes you you.

Believing Is Seeing

During Week One of this makeover, you learned about the power of your beliefs and your attitude. Now in this last week, we come full circle. If you only take one thing to heart from this makeover, please let it be this—*your future is determined by how you perceive yourself today.* Seeing is not believing; believing is seeing. If you have an unwavering view of yourself as capable, strong, beautiful, loving, healthy, and smart, then that is exactly what you will be.

By now you should be perceiving yourself as a competent woman, completely able to manage her home and family and live a healthy, productive, and fulfilling life. Every positive change in your life will begin and end with your self-perception. That is the tipping point. You can set a schedule to clean your house, but until you perceive yourself as someone who deserves a clean home, then you won't be able to change. You can try to change your diet and lose weight, but until you perceive yourself as someone who is healthy and attractive, the weight won't budge. All of the external activities that you are involved in are inferior to the image that you carry within yourself. It all comes down to how you perceive yourself. The person you imagine is the person you will become.

How Big Is Your World?

What do you think is possible? What do you think is impossible? It is your mind that sets the boundaries for what you accomplish in life — not your body, your financial situation, where you live, or who you know. This is a biggie for most moms, especially when we constantly criticize how we raise our kids, how we keep house, and, most especially, how we look. You are the only one who can define what you are capable of accomplishing. So how big is your world? What do you want to do with your life? Your health? Your family? Your home? This makeover is just the beginning of your pursuit of the life you feel you deserve. If you feel that you deserve only the best, then that is exactly what will come your way.

Only the Best Will Do

The more you love and esteem yourself, the pickier you will become about what you are willing to accept. When you love yourself completely, then a natural consequence of this is to want only the very best. The higher you value yourself, the higher your standards will be. There is a good reason that champion racehorses are fed only the highest grade of food and winning race cars have only the best fuel pumped into them. You treat a winner the way a winner needs to be treated. How do you treat yourself? What are your standards? By now, you should consider yourself a winner. So treat yourself as a winner.

◉ **Your Champion Home:** Love your home. No matter how big, small, old, or new, you should love it completely. When you have a positive and healthy image of your home, then you are willing to accept only the very best within its walls. It will be clean and organized because you treat a winner the way a winner needs to be treated. You will see clutter as something that junks up your house and will be more than willing to let it go. You will fill it with energy and beauty because that is what it deserves. And that is the home that *you* deserve.

◉ **Your Champion Health:** Love your body. It has carried you through life this far and nourished and protected your babies. Regardless of size, appearance, or performance, your body should be loved right now. The positive image you have of your body will inspire you to nourish it with only the best food and to give it daily exercise to pump up your energy level and strengthen your muscles. It's a winning relationship: You love your body. You give your body the best treatment. Your body loves you back. Nothing positive can come out of a negative image. Phrases such as "I'm fat" or "I'm ugly" are toxic and have no place in your vocabulary. If you want positive changes, begin with a positive image.

◉ **Your Champion Family:** Love your family. The way you feel and talk about your husband and children will be reflected back on you. I have been with women who harshly criticize their family members. Their kids are lazy and ungrateful. Their husbands are overbearing and inconsiderate. What these women don't realize is that by saying these things, they are facilitating this reality. Believe

"There is no truth.
There is only
perception."

— GUSTAVE
FLAUBERT

in your family and see the very best in them. Fuel your family with positive words and an optimistic attitude. This doesn't mean you need to keep your frustrations buried within you. But be fair in your judgments and try not to jump to negative conclusions. As a mom, your opinion carries a lot of weight. For your family members, especially your children, you are the mirror by which they perceive themselves. What image are you reflecting?

◎ **Your Champion Life:** Love yourself. This is where it all begins. Loving yourself will have a positive effect on every area of your life, your home, your family, your health, *everything.*

Why So Desperate?

When you have a negative self-image, you often feel as if you don't have enough, you don't do enough, and you are not enough. This results in a feeling of desperation. You need more and more in order to feel complete. Unfortunately, we live in a society of desperate housewives. But true fulfillment only happens when we embrace every aspect of who we are and love ourselves completely — not when we reach a certain level but right now, just as we are.

Don't fall into the desperation trap. No one likes a desperate housewife, not even the housewife. That negative self-image affects

TOTAL MOM TIP
**Double
the Blessing**

Make a habit of complimenting yourself or speaking empowering phrases aloud around your children. Saying things such as, "I feel great today!", "I am so proud of myself!"; and "I can do it!" not only strengthens your self-image but also sets a precedent for your children to follow. That's definitely something to keep in mind the next time you look in a full-length mirror and are tempted to berate your thighs!

everything. You have little children who are keenly watching you to find out how to relate to themselves. Give them something solid to build on, not a shaky foundation of desperation. When you feel that negative self-image rearing its ugly head, then start replacing the desperation with appreciation. Instead of focusing on everything that may be lacking, consciously focus on everything that is complete. A little bit of gratitude can do wonders.

Perfection Perception

The more you dwell on being perfect, the more you set yourself up for failure. Don't try to be the perfect wife and mother. That woman doesn't exist! Instead set your sights on becoming the constantly improving wife and mother — now that's something you can sink your teeth into. When you have a healthy self-image, every day presents a new challenge and a new opportunity. You can succeed and you can fail, but always choose to go forward. You are willing to try because you know that the prize is within your reach. And you know that you deserve the best life possible. Why? Because you love yourself — the good, the bad, and everything in between.

Week Six, Day One: Daily Exercises

1. In your journal, write down at least twenty positive things about yourself. No more than five of these attributes should be physical. Think deep and give yourself some credit.

2. Go back in your journal to the exercises you completed on Week One, Day One. This is the list of *should*s that you made — all of those things that bug you. As you look it over, you will probably find that you listed plenty of things that bug you on a personal level. When you come across these, ask yourself if they result from a positive self-image or a negative one. For example, if you want to lose weight because you want to be healthier, then that is a positive *should*. If you want to lose weight to fit that perfect image that you see in the glam mags, then you're going to be one desperate housewife (airbrush artists only work on photographs, not real bodies).

Let yourself cross some things off your list. As you become a more confident and competent mom, you will find that you need fewer and fewer superficial things to be content. You may also find that during these past weeks, you have accomplished many of the *should*s that you listed at the beginning of the makeover. Spend some time doing this exercise. Cross off your accomplishments and anything else on the list that no longer applies. After you have done this, you will be left with some goals to work toward.

Meditate on This

If you are like most people, when you think of meditation, you think of donning a robe and twisting up like a pretzel, all in the pursuit of inner tranquillity. Well, if you just have a hankering for robes, then go ahead and slip into a nice chenille one, but there's no need to go overboard. Don't let the word *meditation* scare you away from an activity that can increase your mental acuity, improve your physical health, lower your stress level, and, overall, help you be a better mommy. Yes, meditation can do all of that and more.

If the Spirit Moves You

Many people shy away from meditation because of the spiritual implications. Although traditional meditation does have its roots in spiritual practice, modern meditation is whatever you make of it. It can be a spiritual experience, but it certainly is not limited to that. It is simply a way of relaxing and centering yourself. Meditation is actually defined as contemplating, thinking, or pondering, and you certainly don't need divine intervention to do any of that.

In its simplest form, meditation is a tool just like any other, and it can be manipulated in whatever way you choose. You can use it to enlighten your spirit or commune with a higher power, or to lower your stress level and help you be a more focused mother. How you use it is up to you, but the important thing is to *use* it.

Anyone and Everyone

Let's get one thing straight. If *I* can meditate, *anyone* can meditate! I can't stand to slow down, physically or mentally. My mind never rests. As a matter of fact, I'm not even through one project before I am planning the next one. I always assumed that I just didn't have the personality to meditate. I thought I had to empty my head in order to meditate, and I didn't even want to try. I have a difficult time even focusing my thoughts, much less clearing them out. I thought meditation would be a waste of time.

But I was wrong. Meditation works with every personality. It improves your health, both physically and mentally. If your thought process is more erratic, like mine is, meditation helps you focus, which in turn helps you become more productive with your time.

How to Meditate

Step One: Dress in something nonbinding and sit in a comfortable position, preferably on a floor cushion. If you prefer to sit on a chair, that's fine. Don't worry if you can't sit cross-legged. The important thing is to be comfortable, so if you sit on the floor, just sit as close to cross-legged as possible.

Step Two: Make sure your back is straight and perfectly aligned, like a roll of coins. If you slump, you can begin to feel sluggish. Good posture will help you remain alert, which is very important.

Step Three: Rest your hands in a relaxed position. You can either place them palms up on your knees or rest them palms up on your lap with one inside the other and thumbs touching. Make sure they are being held in a comfortable position.

Step Four: Lower your head just a bit and gaze downward. You don't want your eyes wide open because this can lead to too much mental excitement. You also don't want to close your eyes because this can cause mental sluggishness. Let your eyelids droop a bit and lower your gaze, perhaps focusing on your hands or a few feet in front of you.

Step Five: Hold your mouth slightly open and your shoulders even. Roll your shoulders forward, around, back, and down to release the tension that you hold in that area of your body and then relax them.

Step Six: First become aware of all the thoughts running through your head. Usually, your mind is full of distractions. This is the time to acknowledge this confusion, but don't try to start sorting stuff out. Just give your head time to float along from one subject to the next without any pressure to process any of it.

Step Seven: Calm your mind by turning your thoughts toward your breathing. Without changing your pattern, just focus on the breath going in, filling up your lungs, and then going out. As you exhale, imagine that you are breathing out all stress, bitterness, and disturbance. As you inhale, imagine that you are breathing in contentment, appreciation, and joy. You can visualize it even better if you imagine your exhale as black smoke and your inhale as white light that fills your lungs and embraces your heart.

Step Eight: Continue this conscious breathing until you feel refreshed, alert, and fully blessed. Now your thoughts are focused, your mind is clear, and you are able to handle anything those kids can throw at you! Aim for at least five minutes of daily meditation to begin with, gradually increasing the duration by a few minutes every week. Your AM routine is an ideal time to meditate because the house should be relatively still and quiet, a perfect time to focus your thoughts and prepare for the day.

Tips: If you are having a difficult time remaining alert, then consciously breathe in through your nose and out through your mouth. If you are having a difficult time focusing, then you can gently hum or repeat a soothing mantra, such as "om."

DIY Meditations

Motherhood calls for some unconventional methods here and there, and meditation is certainly no exception. We don't always have an hour to sit in solitude (if only). But if something is important enough, we can always find a way to squeeze in a few minutes here and there. Meditation doesn't have to be an all-or-nothing activity. You can customize it to fit your lifestyle. Maybe you can do some walking meditation, one of my favorites, where you focus on your breathing as you walk along a quiet path.

Meditation Lowers Your Mommy Stress

Stress and motherhood go together like mall perms and split ends. Every mom out there knows what stress does to a mom. You snap at your kids. You lose your focus. You get nothing accomplished. And your husband definitely gets the raw end of the deal. Meditation is an excellent way to reduce that stress and, in turn, make you more relaxed with your family and more productive with your time. Stress is inevitable, but by taking the time to meditate, you can more effectively handle it by letting go of negative emotions and channeling your energy in a more productive direction. Stress is often caused by too many tasks overwhelming you at once or by a task that is inaccurately perceived to be beyond your abilities. Meditation helps by improving your ability to sort and organize your thoughts, perceptions, and reactions. And the effects of meditation linger throughout the day. So even when you are not meditating, you can still reap the benefits.

**TOTAL MOM TIP
The Magic
Eight Breath**

Squeeze in a mini-meditation during a stoplight by using a breathing technique I call "the Magic Eight Breath." Count slowly to eight while inhaling deeply during the first two counts, holding your breath for the next four counts, and exhaling completely during the last two counts. Repeat this until the light turns green or until you feel refreshed and centered.

Remember those breathing exercises during childbirth class? *That* was meditation. The purpose was to help you think beyond the pain that your body was going through and sort through the experience. Now, if you thought that childbirth was irritating, just imagine when one child dumps a bowl of cereal on the floor, another is complaining about not being allowed to wear a miniskirt to the mall, the phone rings but you can't find it, the soup scorches on the stove, and your toddler gets into the craft glue. A situation like that calls for some serious stress-handling ability, and meditation can help you achieve it.

Meditation Helps You Focus

As moms, we often handle so many things on our to-do lists that we lose focus of why we have chosen this career in the first place. Meditation gives us a reason to pause and regain focus. Understanding the reason behind what you are doing often gives you enough energy, stamina, and

"Only in quiet waters do things mirror themselves undistorted. Only in a quiet mind is adequate perception of the world."

— HANS MARGOLIUS

persistence to actually follow through with it. That's true with any goal, whether it's getting healthy, saving money, cleaning your house, or being a better mom. If you can clearly visualize why you have set a goal, then you increase your chances of reaching it.

Meditation helps you pause to focus on that vision you have for yourself. You have chosen to be a Total Mom, a woman who is devoted to her family, her home, and the pursuit of an abundant and fulfilling life. But sometimes things can get a bit cloudy, and your focus gets lost in the haze of living. Meditation is a way to pull you back on course. It helps you gain proper perspective and understand why it is you do what you do. To the untrained eye, it may seem as if you are just trying to keep your kids and house under control, but you know that you are doing something much, much more. You are establishing a legacy and creating a future. You are providing a sense of home and family. Pausing during the day for a reality check will help you keep your perspective in line. Meditation helps you see beyond the temporal to the eternal and live in harmony with that vision in focus.

The simple act of pausing to center yourself helps you become more mindful of your choices and how you are living them. Moods are floating around, ungrounded and unjustified. A state of mindfulness is living with your eyes wide open. It is fully sensing and absorbing your world so that you can better navigate through it. It is not just hearing, but listening; not just seeing, but understanding. Moods react. Mindfulness responds. Meditation will help you pause long enough to get in that state of awakened mindfulness. Just a few moments of solitude with yourself is enough to help you release the moods that so often dictate reactions and focus on what really matters.

Mind, Body, Spirit

Meditation is one activity that benefits your entire self—mind, body, and spirit. It reduces your stress level and your blood pressure, and has been shown to improve cognitive brain functioning. Meditation also helps you spiritually by allowing you to step away from worldly demands for just a moment and affirm your purpose in this world. It can be an excellent time to visit with God — to pour out your worries and surrender a temporal will for an eternal one. Your spirit can be molded in glorious ways if you just pause long enough to let it happen.

Week Six, Day Two: Daily Exercises

1. In your journal, flip back to Week One, Day Two, where you created a two-page spread full of pictures and quotes that illustrates the vision you have for yourself. You should have left some blank spots here and there to fill in later. Take some time now to look through magazines, books, or Web sites to get a few more illustrations for your page. Make sure they are pictures and words that capture the wonderful, fulfilling, and exciting life that you deserve, and glue them on to these two pages.

2. Take a few minutes this morning or sometime during the day to meditate. It may feel a bit awkward at first, but keep in mind that there is no mystery to it. It's just a time of solitude and peace. When you meditate, open your journal to your two-page spread and place it on the floor a few feet in front of you so that it is in your line of vision while you focus on your breathing. Absorb this vision with every inhalation and let the anxieties go with every exhalation.

Your Child's Real Needs

Every child, no matter what age, has basic needs. I'm not talking food, shelter, and plenty of good books. You already know enough to supply those. I'm talking about the deep needs that sometimes get glossed over in our culture. Children are born with a beautiful desire for life and have an intrinsic knowledge that commonly exceeds our perception. The best thing we can do for our children is to meet these basic needs and then stand back and watch the beauty unfold.

The Need for Power

I have found that many people grossly underestimate a child's need for power. Most of the "power struggles" that parents complain about are the result of not acknowledging this very basic need at the outset. A child needs to feel in control of her life, as if her choices actually make a difference and her world will bend to her touch. Primal? Yes. Do we all share this same need? Absolutely. When we feel as if we do not have power over the course of our lives, hopelessness and bitterness set in. We all have our own power struggles—a child's struggles are no less significant than the ones we face.

Too many times we fall into the "Me, Mommy! You, Child!" frame of mind. Respect your child and allow him to feel a sense of power over his world. Instead of demanding a certain behavior, help him understand why it may be the best choice. Speak with your child like you would with a friend, gathering opinions and coming up with solutions together. Respecting your child, honoring his opinions, and empowering him does not lessen your role as a mother. Remember, you are not running a dictatorship; you're managing a family.

TOTAL MOM TIP
Power Outage

Power struggles are never worth it, but sometimes they present the most teachable moments. Your children are not just struggling with exerting power over an issue; they are also watching to see how you respond to conflict. Avoid raising your voice or threatening in any way. Instead, try following this step-by-step power outage.

Step One: Pause, take a deep breath, and blow out the frustration.

Step Two: Explain your understanding and show that you respect his emotions (e.g., "It's really fun to throw sand, and I know you really want to do that. It frustrates you when I say that you can't.").

Step Three: Explain what is *expected* of him, the *reason* behind it, and the *consequence* of his action (e.g., "You need to stop throwing sand because it could get in someone's eyes. If you continue doing it, you won't be able to play in the sandbox anymore.").

Step Four: Make sure he understands you and can effectively communicate back to you what you explained to him (e.g., "Are you allowed to throw sand? *No.* "What will happen if you choose to do that?" *I won't be able to play in the sandbox.*).

Step Five: Consistently enforce the consequences so he can learn to make better choices. This is not an exact procedure, merely an effective way to handle power struggles. The point is to demonstrate understanding, show respect, explain the situation, and be consistent.

The Need for Acceptance

A child needs to know that no matter what her personality, behavior, talents, or abilities are, she is absolutely accepted for who she is. This is mothering with no strings attached. Your child must feel that she can always get a hug, a loving conversation, and an attitude from you that says, "I enjoy being in your presence," without having to earn it.

When times get tough and the behavior becomes challenging (which it will), forget about sticking to your guns. Put the guns down and stretch out your arms instead. See the behavior, not your child, as unacceptable and help her become aware of the difference. It is your job to help your child grow up with the unshakable knowledge that she is always accepted and always unconditionally loved by you, from now to eternity. Nothing she can ever do will change that, and she needs to know this in the depths of her spirit. Her choices may frustrate you at times, even cause you pain, and you do not have to accept those choices. But you must always accept her.

The Need for Breathing Room

We live in a culture that is jam-packed from morning to night. Our schedules, homes, minds, and lives are filled with so much stuff we can hardly navigate around it all. From soccer practice to music lessons to art class to day camp, our children's days are crammed full. As moms, we are constantly bombarded with what a "good mother" does and often find ourselves subconsciously subscribing to a philosophy that we are somehow shortchanging our children if we don't provide them with every opportunity possible. Instead of developing their skills and abilities, our children's schedules often become a manifestation of our own inadequacies. As a result, meals are eaten on the run, little time is spent together as a family, weekends are spent doing the "soccer mom shuffle," and our children have little to no room in their lives just to play, exist, and simply breathe in life.

Sometimes the best gift you can give your child is not more instruction but more room to develop his own abilities. A child needs to explore and discover, and he needs free time to do this. True genius usually does not occur in the classroom. It happens spontaneously in the backyard with a field guide, over a box of Legos, or through the simple medium of pencil and paper. Don't think for one minute that you are doing a poor job as a mom by not enrolling your child in the submersion French program or weekly toddler gymnastics classes. Quit prodding your child. Enjoy him and let him enjoy himself.

> **TOTAL MOM TIP**
> **Kid**
> **Logic**
>
> Keep in mind that children in no way, shape, or form operate by the same methods that we employ. Ease up and relax with the medium for exploration that your child has chosen. So what if he prefers to work in Scotch tape rather than clay, or paint with glue rather than watercolors? Resist the temptation to apply your grown-up logic to his kid-size world.

The Need for Security

Nothing beats the feeling of a warm blanket when it's cold outside or a strong hand to hold when the path is rocky. All of us have a deep need for security. We long to feel safe in an unsure world, and our children are no different. Parents frequently fall into the trap of equating their child's fears and insecurities with their own. However, the size of the event does not determine the level of anxiety. The first day of preschool can be just as scary for a child as the first day on the job is for an adult.

We are not overprotecting our children by providing them with unlimited amounts of security. Pushing them out of the nest does nothing to develop their wings. It only teaches them that this world is a scary place and that their fears are completely warranted. Believe me, when they are ready, they will fly—with complete freedom and confidence. It is not our job to force our children to face their fears. It is our job, however, to give them the security of knowing that they are not facing their fears alone. Throughout your children's lives, you do not need to clear the path before them and you do not need to shove them down it. You merely need to stay close behind and back them up.

The Need to Feel Treasured

Your children are a gift. Don't ever let a day go by without somehow confirming this. Your children need to know that your life is greater, richer, fuller simply because of them. There are so many ways to show them how much you treasure them. You can treasure them with the simple gift of undivided attention. Give them your full attention when they speak to you, with eyes on them, ears hearing every word. Treasure

TOTAL MOM TIP
Let Go
Last

It's important not only to embrace your children frequently but also to be the last to let go. Make a habit of holding your child (no matter how old, whether two or twenty) until she lets go. When she wraps herself around you, stop what you are doing and hug her right back. And don't let go, even if you have a hundred other things to do or if you are running ten minutes late to a conference. The most important thing at that moment in time is your child's need to feel loved and treasured. Hug her back, hold it, and be the last to let go.

them by showing them that no *thing* is ever more important than they are. Paint spills, windows break, carpets get destroyed, and walls mysteriously get colored on. These are all *things,* just *things.* A dining room chair is easy to repair; a child's wounded spirit is not. Show them you treasure them by operating on their time, not yours. Slow down enough to really appreciate who they are. That is the true treasure.

The Need to Fail

I am constantly astounded at a child's natural propensity to learn. From the moment that little baby takes his first step, falls to the ground, gets back up again, and takes those final steps into outstretched arms, he has learned that his efforts produce results. He has also learned that sometimes you need to fall on your fanny a few times to get where you want to go. This simple model is the key to success in life — failures are often the most effective means of learning, and persistence always pays off.

Children are often denied this lesson today. Our society goes to extremes to even the playing field and remove failure from the picture. Failure is uncomfortable, there's no doubt about that. But we all need to realize that it is a very necessary part of a successful life. It is not our task as moms to eliminate failure. It is our task to teach our children that failure is a part of life, one that should never be feared. We need to teach them too that, on the flip side of the coin, persistence always results in success. Delayed gratification is a wonderful gift to give to your children. What joy they will have in life when they learn that the best things are worth working for, saving for, and waiting on. Whether it's that first car or that first kiss. Instant gratification is euphoric, but the lesson is never learned and the pleasure never lasts. As a Total Mom, you don't need to make your children's lives perfect. Instead, you need to adequately equip your children to handle the inevitable imperfections that come with it.

> "The hardest part of raising a child is teaching them to ride bicycles. . . . A shaky child on a bicycle for the first time needs both support and freedom. The realization that this is what the child will always need can hit hard."
> — SLOAN WILSON

Week Six, Day Three: Daily Exercises

1. Glance through your calendar. Do you need to cut back on some of the activities in your children's schedules? Are their activities mirroring their desires or merely filling up their time? If there are activities that you can cut out of their schedules, cut them.

2. Look back in your journal to Week One, Day Three. In the second exercise, you listed some empowering words and phrases that you can use with your children. Are you using them? Are you building up your children daily? Are your actions mirroring your words?

3. In your journal, write down a list of ways that you can make your child feel treasured—a love note, a trip out together, a "date night." Remember, the best gift is *you,* not *things.* After you make the list, pick one or two ideas and put them into action. If it is a love note, then go ahead and write it. If it is a trip out together, then adjust your schedule to make room for it today or tomorrow. If it is a date night, then write it on the calendar and make it happen.

Keeping It Up

Y ou're almost there. The ribbon is stretched across the path before you, and you are just about to break through it. But what happens next? When you close this book and your six weeks are up, what are you going to do? How do you keep up the pace? The thing you have to keep in mind is that the Total Mom Makeover jump-starts you into a new way of living. It's not a project with a beginning, a middle, and an end. It's a process that continues to shape your life long after the six weeks are over. But how do you keep living the Total Mom life? It all comes down to life choices, daily choices, even moment-by-moment choices. Every effort you put into building the life you deserve will reward you in amazing ways. In other words, this makeover is just the beginning.

Operate on a Different Wavelength

You know by now that the level of success in your life depends upon the standards that you set for yourself and the reality that you are willing to accept. It's true today, tomorrow, and for the rest of your life. You have stretched your boundaries, and life exists in the realm of possibilities. That's the way it should be. What is possible for you in life depends upon what you believe is possible. And this belief creates a vision. The vision becomes your reality. And your reality dictates all your life choices.

One way to keep that momentum going is to accept only the reality that mirrors your new life. The Total Mom life is your new wavelength of operation. Negative junk will attack you constantly. You know as well as I do that the norm for many people can be pretty depressing, discouraging, and disturbing. I've been around moms who can't seem to say one positive or happy word. This is not your mode of operation anymore. You are living on a new frequency. Imagine that everything you see, hear, think, and do exists as wavelengths flowing into and out of your life. One way to keep up the pace of your new life is to acknowledge and "process" only those wavelengths that support you. If it is not building you up, then it's most likely tearing you down. Don't let it. You are the one who is operating the controls, so tune in to the good stuff.

Step Out of Your Comfort Zone

If you are not living out of your comfort zone once in a while, then you're not really living. The "uncomfortable zone" is where all of the success stories are written. The comfort zone feels good; the uncomfortable zone feels like sliding downhill on sandpaper naked. It's rough, raw, and gritty, but it's the only path that will get you where you want to go in life.

There are times in life when an opportunity presents itself or another one of those crazy, harebrained ideas strikes you in the middle of the night. You have a choice. You can roll over and go back to sleep, or you can get out of bed and take action. Sometimes you've just got to throw caution to the wind every once in a while and take some risks. But honestly, there really is no safety in nature. Any security we feel is false. If it's not coming down from heaven, then it doesn't really exist. So if you are worried about taking a chance, then forget about it. Life is already a chance, so make it count for something. Step out of your comfort zone, take some risks, get messy, look foolish, fall flat on your face, and then get right back up. It's worth it. After a while, you'll get used to that exhilarating feeling of sliding downhill on sandpaper. Yes, you'll actually become comfortable in your uncomfortable zone!

I love living life to the fullest. And if you have made it all the way to Week Six, then I know that you do, too. Here's a little trick that I always keep in the back of my mind: Be outrageous! Don't wait until you are an old lady to wear a purple dress with a red hat. Do it now! I love telling perfect strangers how wonderful they look or dancing in the rain with my kids or singing in an elevator or anything that verges on the outrageous. Do something simple to start out with—buy a pack of gum and offer the cashier or the customer behind you in line a piece of it or paint a heart on your cheek with lipstick and wear it all day long. Start a habit of behaving a bit outrageously. Life is meant to be fun.

TOTAL MOM TIP
The Outrageous Thing

Go Slo-Mo

The prize is in the journey of life, not the destination. Sometimes in our haste to reach the finish line we forget that motherhood often requires that we operate in slow motion. Families are far too rushed these days, and as the manager of the family, you have to be the one to set the pace. But keep in mind that the pace you set for your family does not necessarily have to mirror the pace you set for yourself.

Being a successful home and family manager requires that you put 110 percent of yourself into the job. It means waking up when you want to sleep in, standing up when you want to sit down. It demands a lot of you, but you will reap the rewards of your efforts in so many ways—a smoothly running home, a happy and healthy family, and an exceedingly productive life. But the pace of your personal life does not need to permeate your entire family. Homes need to operate in slow motion once in a while, especially when those homes are filled with children. And one of the positive results of keeping up the pace of the Total Mom life is that when you get a lot accomplished, you earn the privilege of turning the pace down in order to fully enjoy your family.

Remember to pause long enough to enjoy the slo-mo life. There will always be a hundred things to do, but that doesn't necessarily mean you need to do them right now. Sometimes choosing to stop and relax with your family is the best way to spend your time. Action Skill #7: Do It Now isn't limited to your task list. It applies to your family as well. If you need to take in a movie with the kids, eat some snacks by the pool, or try out the new restaurant, then maybe you need to do it now. Learn how to judge what is most important. Sometimes we need to push forward in our lives, but there are other times when the best choice is to hold back and soak it all in.

"Life moves pretty fast. If you don't stop and look around once in a while, you could miss it."
— FERRIS BUELLER, *FERRIS BUELLER'S DAY OFF*

Put Pen to Paper

Another way to keep up the Total Mom Life is to learn the value of making lists. Putting goals and tasks down on paper accomplishes a remarkable thing. It puts action toward that goal and sets a plan in motion. That is one reason why you have been keeping a journal for the past six weeks—to develop a strategy and follow through with it. Keeping lists is key to being a Total Mom. You should have a Pantry Planner posted in your kitchen. That is your list for groceries and other items that you need to pick up when you run errands. You should also have a day planner. That is your list for appointments and other activities. You should also have a monthly calendar of meals posted in your kitchen. That is your list for family dinners, so you don't have to worry about facing a bunch of empty stomachs and wondering eyes when six o'clock rolls around. When an idea pops in your head, or the kids request an outing, or you realize that you only have one roll of toilet paper left in the house, don't just let that thought swim around in your head. Put it down on paper.

Fill Up by Pouring Out

No matter how much effort you put into your life, you will never be truly fulfilled until you pour yourself out into the lives of others. Need is everywhere, and true greatness occurs when you are able to give of yourself. It may sound odd, but one way to make sure that your needs are continually being met is to continually try to meet the needs of others. It's so much easier to lift yourself up if you are focused on lifting up others in the process.

You are not playing this game of life solo. We're all on the same team. Moms are intrinsically aware of this fact because we can easily go from morning to night without giving a single thought to our own care and keeping. But true selflessness does not translate to putting yourself dead last. On the contrary, selflessness happens when you are able to be a totally fulfilled individual and then let that energy pour out into the lives of those around you. It's true with everyone. We can be more for our children, our husbands, our friends, and the world around us when we are more for ourselves. And when we are living up to our full potential, that's when we truly have something to offer this world.

You may think that you have little to offer. The needs are so great out there, and you are only one person. Recall the beauty of a starlit night. The sky would be awfully bleak without any stars, but as each one glimmers in the night sky, the heavens become jeweled with glory. Be a jewel in this world by pouring out your blessings to the world around you. You can do anything—whether it's tutoring kids, volunteering in a soup kitchen, or shopping for elderly people. Find something you can do and do it.

It takes a certain amount of trust to let go of our time, money, energy, and possessions. But life works in a fluid manner. Blessings cannot pool up and stagnate. If they do, they are no longer blessings, but trappings. If you really want to be blessed, then be a blessing. When you do, you will experience fulfillment of supernatural proportions. If you try to hold on to things, you are left feeling empty. But if you let go and give of yourself, then you will feel totally and completely full. It's one of those incredible benefits that goes along with the Total Mom life—you fill up by pouring out!

Week Six, Day Four: Daily Exercises

1. What are some of the ways you can step out of your comfort zone? Is there a goal that you tossed out or a long-lost dream you would like to pursue? Write these goals and dreams down in your journal.

2. Look back in your journal at Week One, Day Four. You listed several ways to apply action skills to your home, health, family, and life. Are you covering all your bases? Are you balancing fast pace with slow motion? If you are neglecting some areas, then now is the time to pursue them. What do you need to take action on? As you look over the action skills, think of ways to apply them to the dreams and goals that you listed in the above exercise and write those down as well. Schedule the steps you need to take in order to follow through.

3. In your journal, make a list of some ways that you can give of yourself. My daughters and I go to a retirement home every other

week to give the ladies manicures and makeup. The ladies all love it, but I honestly think that my daughters and I are the ones reaping the blessing. It feels so good to give away your time, energy, and possessions. Remember, you don't have to take on anything huge; no one is expecting you to end world hunger by next week. Just think of some viable ways to make this world a better place and write them down. Then pick one and put some action behind it. Set the date and make a phone call or do whatever you need to do to get the ball rolling.

Living in the Peaks

Back when Maslow first came up with the hierarchy of needs, he cited that the ability to have peak experiences was one of the characteristics of a completely developed individual. Peak experiences are those moments in life when everything seems to come together in one blissful moment. They are the "mountaintop experiences" of life when we transcend the here and now and feel intense joy and well-being, when all is right with the world and we are overwhelmed with a sense of unity and awe. Think back to when you held that precious baby for the first time—that was a peak experience! Immense joy just wells up within you, and the stress and worry just fade away as we catch a glimpse into the eternal. It's as if the world around us gets blurry and life suddenly comes into focus. Peak experiences are those moments we want to savor and visit in our memories again and again.

But the thing about peaks is that you eventually come back down to reality. The diaper leaks, the bill arrives, and the chorus of angels suddenly exits stage left. The mountaintop that you were just standing on crumbles beneath you as you go tumbling down. The peak experience was so deliciously perfect that you still have the delectable taste in your mouth when you get back into the daily grind. Those peak experiences are great, aren't they? And wouldn't it be nice if they just lasted a bit longer or came a bit more frequently? Well, now that you are a Total

Mom, I'll let you in on a little secret: Your whole life can be a peak experience!

Peak experiences don't have to be few and far between. Many people have this idea that wonderful feelings and blissful experiences happen by the luck of the draw and that if we live right, cross our fingers, and treat Lady Luck nicely, then maybe, just maybe, one of those raindrops will fall upon our heads.

Happiness doesn't work that way. It's not a random event, not at all. Happiness is a choice. And if you want to live in bliss, then you need to make the right choice at every turn in the path. The joy and satisfaction that you derive from life is directly related to the choices you make. It's not the effort you put into it, but where you apply it. It's not the time you spend, but how you spend it. If you want to live in the peaks, then you need to make the choices that will get you there and keep you there. Don't be afraid to take a risk. You'll never know the joy of living in the peaks if you are afraid to climb up the mountains.

It's What's Inside That Counts

It's not what happens to you that determines your life path; it's how you respond to what happens to you. This is one of those choices that will keep you in the peaks. How are you going to respond to circumstances? Some circumstances may very well be out of your control, but how you respond to them is always in your control. Don't ever let any circumstance rob you of power. You have ultimate control if you choose it. It is your right and your privilege to choose joy over sorrow, peace over chaos, and strength over weakness.

Living in the peak of life doesn't happen when everything goes your way. It is not dependent upon external events at all. Instead, peak experiences originate within you. They exist solely in your perception. Because of this, your life can easily be a peak experience if you choose to perceive it that way. If you still believe that you will be happy when you "have it all," then I'm afraid you may be setting yourself up for a very disappointing life. As soon as you get what you want, there will be one more thing you need in order to feel satisfied. The pursuit of happiness through external fulfillment is a race that has no finish line, no happy ending. If you want true contentment, then it needs to come from within. Don't rely on stuff to make you happy; rely on your choices. You can choose happiness today without waiting for it to come with an event, a milestone, a possession, or an accomplishment. Look beyond your external circumstances to foster joy, peace, and strength within you.

TOTAL MOM TIP
Forty-eight
Hours

When something especially nauseating happens—your car gets totaled, your husband loses his job, all of the plumbing in the new house leaks, your health insurance refuses payment—there's no getting around the fact that it feels pretty miserable. If you are anything like me, even with all of the attitude work in the world, you will still have that sinking feeling gnawing at your belly, and there's practically nothing you can do about it. Take a deep breath and just give it forty-eight hours. These inevitable situations are just a natural part of the ebb and flow of life. Breathe through it and give yourself a good two days before you make any rash decisions or judgments. Forty-eight hours can do wonders to chase away the misery fog so you can see clearly and think logically through the situation. Let time do its work. You'll be surprised at what forty-eight hours can do to alter your perception.

Be You

Most people go through life living it backward. They want a lot of stuff *so that* they can be free to do what they want *so that* they can discover who they are. However, it never works that way, and most people don't figure that out until it's too late. Actually, it's quite the opposite. First, you need to discover who you are. Then, by discovering who you are, you grant yourself the freedom to do what you want. And when you find this passion and live it out in your life, the world responds. The stuff comes later, but by then, it doesn't matter nearly as much as you thought it did. It's just superfluous, a fringe benefit of the magnificence of discovering your passion.

Living in the peaks can only happen when you live *your* life and nobody else's. There is no magic to discovering who you are. If you start out on a journey to find yourself, then you will go around in circles until you get right back where you started, probably just as confused, or perhaps more so, than you were when you began. You are what you are living right now. And the real beauty of it is that it is always changing and evolving. You do not have to be defined in any way, because you are a growing individual.

Living in the peaks means embracing yourself just as you are, wherever you are in the process of life. Give it your all and don't shortchange yourself by being less than the very best. Instead of searching for yourself, develop what you have and where you are right now. Be the very best wife, mom, and woman that you can possibly be. Don't waste time searching for yourself out there somewhere. Mine the jewels that you already possess within you. You can struggle along the path of life as a second-rate version of someone else, or you can live in the peaks as the best version of yourself. Celebrate who you are, without limits, without definitions, without labels. Simply, you.

"Each morning when I awake, I experience again a supreme pleasure—that of being Salvador Dalí."
— SALVADOR DALÍ

Keep Climbing

You can ask any mountain climber about the crux of a climb. The crux is the most difficult portion of an ascent. If you can make it through the crux, then the mountain is yours. But that's a big "if." The crux is that portion of a climb that weeds out the winners from the wannabes. The winners make it through and look at the world from the peak of the climb. The wannabes gripe and complain that the climb is too difficult and just hang out at base camp. Sometimes, those peaks can be quite elusive.

But life is not meant to be easy. It is meant to be lived. There are going to be some awfully severe cruxes that will threaten to keep you from living in the peaks. But when the climb gets tough, the climber focuses only on her very next step. She knows in the back of her mind that the little steps add up and that the peak is there waiting for her. She doesn't think about how many feet she has to go before she reaches the top. She concentrates on getting a good hold and inching forward. Even if the movement is small, it is not insignificant, for she is not letting go.

There are plenty of cruxes in a mom's life, times when the winners are weeded out from the wannabes. It's important to see that even on those days when we feel as if we have made no forward movement, we still continue to hang on. Don't try to focus on the end of the road. Just focus on your very next move. Make it a positive one. Even if it is inch by inch, you will make it through those times and come out on the other side stronger, more confident, and more determined than ever.

Remember that every positive motion is building you into the mom and the woman that you were designed to be. This is your shot. It's your life. Don't waste any more time at base camp. The view is better and the air cleaner when you live in the peaks. No, it won't be easy. Nothing worthwhile ever is. But can you think of anything more worthwhile than you? Your home? Your family? It's in your hands. It's your turn to climb—and to win!

Week Six, Day Five: Daily Exercises

1. In your journal, write your name vertically down the left side of the page. Now using each letter, write down a unique and wonderful quality about you. For example, for the first letter of my name, *H*, I might write down "*H*earty laughter" or "*H*ave a beautiful singing voice." You may have done an activity like this in grade school. But you're all grown up now, and it's more fun than ever. Have a good time with this!

2. In your journal, flip back to Week One, Day Five. You wrote down specific ways that you could respond to situations with a powerful attitude. Have you been practicing it? Your life has evolved a bit since then, and you may have an entirely new set of challenges. Is there an area in your life where you have a tendency to revert to an unhealthy or negative state? Imagine some effective ways to manage this situation. For example, you may struggle with laziness and fall into a pattern of not exercising. An effective way to deal with this may be to get a fitness partner. Write down some solutions to these challenges in your journal and act on them so that you can stay on the right track.

Total Mom Life Plan

Congratulations! You did it! You broke through that ribbon, and now you are running for the peak! Let this be the beginning of a totally new and incredibly fulfilling life on all levels. You are 100 percent Total Mom! Now go live the life that you deserve! Every mountain climb needs a plan. Here is a game plan to help you freshen up when you feel yourself going through a particularly demanding crux.

Home: Remember to keep up with the weekly cleaning chores. If you miss out on a day, then let it go. If you try to double up on your chores the next day, it might get you discouraged. The house will still be standing next week, and you can get to it then. However, if you feel a sudden burst of energy the next day, then go ahead and do yesterday's chores after you complete the chores for that day.

Keep up with those zones as well. As you de-clutter one zone every week, you will eventually get back around to Zone 1. When you do, just start the cycle all over again. Spend that week doing any de-cluttering, organizing, and deep cleaning that needs to be done (look at things like the ceiling fans or baseboards).

Health: You will skip a workout here and there because that's just the way life goes, especially for a mom who has to meet demands at every turn. Don't get discouraged when that happens. Just get right back into it the very next day. And remember to work exercise into your daily routine. Even if you don't have time for a full-fledged workout, you can at least do some strength training while you pick up the house and step out for a quick twenty-minute walk.

Meditating every morning is ideal, but if that doesn't work for you, aim for small pockets of time here and there. Perhaps you can do a breathing meditation while you walk or spend five minutes meditating instead of twenty.

Keep that B.A.D. C.R.A.P. out of your diet and give yourself and your family the best nutrition possible. Post a chart in your kitchen as a reminder of the foods to avoid. Remember to continually tweak your family dishes to increase nutrition.

Family: Now that you are a Total Mom, you are filled up and fully able to pour your energy into building up the family unit and strengthening your marriage. Remember to focus daily on your relationship with your husband. If things are beginning to slip, then stop it now before it gets any worse. Instead of playing mind games, play some real games. Make a standing date for a fun game of tennis or play a card game after the kids go to bed. The couple that plays together, stays together.

Playing doesn't need to be limited to your marriage. Include the kids as well. Having fun together encourages unity as a family. Go on a screen diet by limiting television, video games, and computer time and replace that time with fun family activities. Perhaps you could start a tradition of one screen-free day every week and schedule different family activities for each one.

Life: You are living a Total Mom life now, but it won't stick if you don't make a conscious decision every day to actively pursue the life that you deserve. Remember to keep up the AM and PM routines. And keep using your journal. Write in it every day and use it to explore new dimensions of yourself.

Get some daily support by checking in with the TotalMom.com to connect with moms who are doing the same thing you are—building a family and a home, living life to the very fullest, and loving every minute of it.

The Sweetest Time

I often get asked how to survive motherhood. Nope, sorry. Wrong question. The real question is how to thrive during motherhood. As you already know, this can be a wonderfully fulfilling time in your life, not just with the family and the home, but with you as well. Don't ever sink so low that you are concerned with surviving. You are better than that. This is the time of your life to think big and dream even bigger. Make wishes, follow your heart, and shake things up a bit. Don't waste another day trying to make it through. Wake up and go after what you want. Sink into bed at night knowing that you gave it your all and that your kids, your husband, your home, and you are better because of it. This can indeed be the sweetest time of your life.

One day, I was out with the children running some errands, when I noticed an elderly couple eyeing us and smiling (as a rule, I get smiles from older people and grimaces from younger ones. I believe this is because age has a way of teaching us what really matters in life). I was busy talking with the little ones and telling them to quit grabbing the candy bars that were strategically placed at their eye level in the checkout aisle, when the couple approached me.

"Are these all your children?" the elderly woman asked.

"Yes, ma'am, every last one of them," I replied.

The man and woman smiled at each other; then she leaned in to me, as if to secretly disclose the wisdom of the ages.

"Honey," she said, "enjoy this time of your life. It's the sweetest time of all."

"Oh, I am," I blithely responded, and then reached down to grab the M&M's out of my son's hand and place them back on the shelf. The elderly couple looked at each other once more and strolled away down the cereal aisle.

At the time I remember thinking that this couple was obviously completely unaware of the horrible state my home was in and the enormous pile of dirty clothes and sheets that was growing mildew in the laundry room. I barely had time to enjoy being a mother between the diapers, the meals, the errands, and the constant cleaning.

But, inevitably, age and experience teach us much more than we can learn from words alone. Back then, I had no idea that the elderly woman in the grocery store was indeed bestowing upon me the wisdom of the ages. I was just not quite prepared at the time to receive it. We always know more looking back than we do looking ahead. And now I understand that this chapter of life, with toddlers spilling their cereal on the floor and crunching it under their tiny toes, little babies wrapped up in cotton blankets and breathing on my neck, little boys jumping on their beds, and little girls putting ribbons in their hair, is indeed the sweetest chapter. And when the fog clears and a hush falls over the household, I can almost taste it. Relish this moment of your life and take the time to gaze into your children's eyes, to make midnight snacks, and to lie on a blanket together and talk about the mysteries of life, like why unicorns aren't at the zoo, why fingers get wrinkly in the bath, and why elderly people always smile at you in the grocery store.

Acknowledgments

A mom is only as good as the people who believe in her.

A huge hug and a big thank-you go to all of the wonderful individuals in my life who helped make this project a reality. William, you were one of the first people to share my vision and stand behind it. Thank you for putting feet to the dream. Tracy, you are meticulous. I love it! Thank you for the time and effort you spent to make this a winner. Mom and Dad, I learned from the best. Thank you for putting up with the drama. Sam and Suanne, you are two of the reasons I married Blair. Thank you for supporting the vision, even when it got pretty dark at times.

And, of course, the best for last—Blair, you are still as sexy as you were when you conveniently jogged past my sunbathing spot in college. Thank you for not giving up and not giving in, even when glue trickled down the side of your face. And thank you to my fantastic children, who taught me everything I know about motherhood—Kelsey, Katie, Kyler, Karis, Korben, Klara, and especially little baby Kenna, whose lullaby for the first six months of her life was the gentle *tap-tap-tap* of my fingers on the keyboard.

TOTAL MOM TIPS

Index